Best-
Negro Spirituals

Complete Lyrics
to 178 Songs of Faith

Compiled and Edited by
Nicole Beaulieu Herder
with Ronald Herder

Foreword by
PAUL T. KWAMI
Director, Fisk University Jubilee Singers

DOVER PUBLICATIONS, INC.
Mineola, New York

DOVER MUSICAL ARCHIVES

Copyright

Bibliographical Note

Best-Loved Negro Spirituals: Complete Lyrics to 178 Songs of Faith is a new work, first published by Dover Publications, Inc. in 2001.

International Standard Book Number

ISBN-13: 978-0-486-41677-9
ISBN-10: 0-486-41677-1

Manufactured in the United States by LSC Communications
41677107   2018
www.doverpublications.com

To
Hayward Cirker
(1917–2000)

Founder of Dover Publications,
who loved the idea of folks getting together to sing the old songs.
This is his book in spirit and design.

FOREWORD

I was a little boy growing up in Ghana when I first heard a group of people singing a moving devotional song. To this day I remember those words and that melody and the way the song was sung. I loved those old songs, little knowing that one day, in America, my professional life would be surrounded by the rich musical tradition of the spiritual—what we once called "plantation songs"—whose roots were in my native Africa.

Although I knew about slavery, my understanding of its effect on people was very limited. It was not until my student days at Fisk that I realized the powerful influence of enslavement on people and their music, and how musical elements traveled from African musical culture to the Americas through the slave trade. Just as Africans in Africa created and performed music to express their feelings, tell stories, entertain one another, accompany their work, and worship God, so did the slaves on colonial America's plantations. While capture and servitude hardened their lives, music and religion remained with them as sources of strength and means of self-preservation and self-expression.

A vast body of songs in the oral tradition was born on the plantation, yet much of this music was lost forever simply because no one wrote it down. The realization soon grew that keeping this vital music alive depended on preservation of the spiritual through performance, and on its proper documentation through scholarly study. The pioneering concert tours of the Fisk University Jubilee Singers since 1871 helped to accomplish the first goal, so positive was their reception in performances of spirituals worldwide, from Edinburgh, London and Berlin to Ceylon, Melbourne and Hong Kong.

This activity was later supported by the exemplary preservation work of scholars John Wesley Work, author of *Folk Song of the American Negro*—one of the earliest serious treatments of the subject—by his son, John Wesley Work II, author of *American Negro Songs and Spirituals,* and by Natalie Curtis-Burlin, whose 1918 publication *Negro Folk-Songs* set a new standard for the precise musical notation of an entirely oral art form. Today, the significant musical literature represented by the single name "spiritual" stands as a unique chapter in America's rich cultural heritage.

PAUL T. KWAMI
Director
Fisk University Jubilee Singers
Spring 2001

NOTES ON THE NEGRO FOLK SONG

These songs, now traditional, were originally extemporaneous. They sprang into life as the expression of an emotion, of an experience, of a hope. The verses were made up as the occasion called for them—and a song was born. As the songs passed from singer to singer and from one locality to another, they took on variants in words and melody; even today, two singers rarely sing a song in exactly the same way. Even as some plants bud from slips instead of from seeds, one song would grow from another instead of from an original source. Thus we often see the root-idea of one spiritual flowering into different form in another; or sometimes we find whole borrowed phrases or vivid imagery cropping out in songs otherwise unrelated.

It is only owing to limited opportunity that so often the highest reaches of poetic imagination—common to most simple people who live close to nature—had to be expressed in the everyday words that formed the vocabulary of the slave-poet. However, this very poverty of means gave birth to a unique poetic quality, poignant with character, quaint and ingenuous, throwing forth imagery with striking simplicity and directness, often using wholly natural symbols common to all races.

Thus the "valley" is the symbolic place of prayer and of sadness and struggle; the "mountain top," that of exaltation; the vision of a "starry crown," a "long white robe," or "silver slippers," elements of a heaven which was the dream of a slave. Touchingly naive—with that simplicity that is the glory of the soul awaiting salvation—is the imagery of a chariot, a "Gospel train," a "freedom train," the "Old Ship of Zion"— elements found in a number of spirituals—racing swiftly to deliverance as joyful voices eagerly urge us to "get on board!"

The verses of "Go Down, Moses"—a spiritual that deserves to rank with the great songs of the world—were born of slavery. In the sorrows of Israel in Egypt, oppressed and in bondage, the Negro drew a natural poetic analogy to his own fate. Rarely did the slave dare to sing openly of slavery or of the hope for any other freedom than that promised by the release of death: through the allegory of the Bible he tells of his firm faith for a like deliverance from the hand of the plantation Pharaoh.

With what few words, and yet how clear-drawn, is the oft-recurring picture of the Lord appearing intimately as a personal liberator . . .

My good Lord's been here,
And He's blessed my soul and gone.

. . . or of Jesus symbolized as a conquering monarch. . .

Ride on, King Jesus, ride on,
No man can hinder Him . . .

Into the spirituals—the prayer-songs of the days of slavery—was poured the aspiration of a race in bondage whose religion, primitive and intense, was their whole hope, sustenance and comfort, and the realm wherein the soul, at least, soared free. At stolen meetings and secret gatherings, the Negroes found outlet for their sorrows, their longings, and their religious ecstasies. No one can hear these songs unmoved, filled as they are with a poetry born of hearts that sang beneath heavy burdens, and of a faith as radiant and certain as the sunrise. The spirituals rank with the great folk music of the world, and are among the loveliest of chanted prayers.

NATALIE CURTIS-BURLIN

Freely adapted from her prefatory materials written for *Negro Folk-Songs*, a part of the Hampton Series, originally published by G. Schirmer, Inc., New York, in 1918, and reprinted in 2001 by Dover Publications

We came to love this vast body of folk poetry as we moved—with great deliberation and even greater respect—through a forest of moving words and striking images. Our problem was not in what to include but rather in how we could possibly *omit* this or that spiritual. It was not easy. The result of our choices—178 spirituals of various forms and poetry—is now in your hands.

The question of written language—particularly the rendering of dialect and variant spellings—was a fundamental issue as we assembled and edited these texts. Faced with a large number of spelling variants among our written sources (few of which were consistent), we decided to present the poetry of the spirituals in plain English, without the traditional "heab'nly Lawd," "chillun," and the like that abound in many texts. While this affects a certain amount of picturesque color of the spiritual's language, it seemed to us a simpler, less arbitrary, presentation of the moving message of songs that "rank with the great folk music of the world," as Natalie Curtis-Burlin observed.

Suzanne Flandreau, Librarian and Archivist for the Center for Black Music Research, Columbia College Chicago, was especially helpful in getting us started. She was gracious and generous in recommending valuable source materials for study, suggesting contacts with professionals currently involved in public performance of the spiritual, and in sharing ideas for this new collection.

Our question to performing professionals—"What music do you program these days?"—initiated us into a basic body of works that, along with classic collections still in print, form the nucleus of our volume. For their sympathetic cooperation and carefully prepared lists of songs, our thanks go to Dr. Marvin Curtis, Fayetteville State University; Professor Clyde Owen Jackson, Tuskegee University; and Paul Kwami, conductor of the legendary Fisk Jubilee Singers, Fisk University, who kindly agreed, as well, to write the foreword to this Dover edition.

Our text sources include Dover reprints of six classic books in the field: John W. Work's *American Negro Songs;* Allen, Ware and Garrison's *Slave Songs of the United States;* Harold Courlander's *Negro Folk Music, U.S.A.;* Lomax and Lomax's *Our Singing Country;* Roland Hayes' *My Favorite Spirituals;* and Natalie Curtis-Burlin's *Negro Folk-Songs: The Hampton Series, Books I–IV, Complete.*

Additional sources include three rare books, currently out of print: *The Story of the Jubilee Singers*—J. B. T. Marsh's account, with music, of the extraordinary pioneering chapter in the spiritual's history; and James Weldon Johnson and J. Rosamond Johnson's *The Book of American Negro Spirituals* and *The Second Book of Negro Spirituals.*

We are indebted, as well, to editor Erskine Peters for the availability for research of his wonderfully comprehensive *Lyrics of the Afro-American Spiritual: A Documentary Collection,* a part of The Greenwood Encyclopedia of Black Music, published by Greenwood Press, Westport, CT, in 1993.

Finally, we take editorial responsibility for the overall content, poetic form, typographical style, spellings, and inconsistencies of the spirituals printed in this volume. The structural oddity of many lyrics (unbalanced or irregular in the conventional sense) was a pleasurable challenge to solve in our own way, as were our decisions to present the more typical stanza/refrain and statement/response lyrics in the clearest way we knew.

NICOLE BEAULIEU HERDER
with RONALD HERDER

Spring 2001

CONTENTS

Titles arranged alphabetically

A Great Camp-Meeting in the Promised Land

1. O, walk together, children
    Don't you get weary,
    Walk together, children,
    Don't you get weary,
    Walk together, children,
    Don't you get weary,
    There's a great camp-meeting in the Promised Land.

2. O, talk together, children, *(etc.)*
3. O, sing together, children, *(etc.)*

    Chorus:
    Going to mourn and never tire,
    Mourn and never tire,
    Mourn and never tire,
    There's a great camp-meeting in the Promised Land.

4. O, get you ready, children, *(etc.)*
5. For Jesus is a-coming, *(etc.)*

    Chorus:
    Going to pray and never tire,
    Pray and never tire,
    Pray and never tire,
    There's a great camp-meeting in the Promised Land.

6. There's a better day a-coming, *(etc.)*
7. O, clap your hands, children, *(etc.)*
8. O, will you go with me? *(etc.)*

    Chorus:
    Going to shout and never tire,
    Shout and never tire,
    Shout and never tire,
    There's a great camp-meeting in the Promised Land.

9. O, feel the Spirit a-moving, *(etc.)*
10. O, now I'm getting happy, *(etc.)*

    Chorus:
    O, fly and never tire,
    Fly and never tire,
    Fly and never tire,
    There's a great camp-meeting in the Promised Land.

Ain't Got Time to Die

Leader & response:

Lord, I keep so busy praising my Jesus,
Ain't got time to die.

'Cause when I'm healing the sick,
Ain't got time to die.

'Cause it takes all my time to praise my Jesus,
Ain't got time to die.

If I don't praise Him, the rocks gonna cry out:
"Glory and honor, glory and honor!"
Ain't got time to die.

Lord, I keep so busy working for the kingdom,
Ain't got time to die.

'Cause when I'm feeding the poor,
I'm working for the kingdom,
And I ain't got time to die.

Lord, I keep so busy serving my Master,
Ain't got time to die.

'Cause when I'm giving my all,
I'm serving my Master,
And I ain't got time to die.

Ain't That Good News!
(1st version)

1. I've got a crown up in the Kingdom,
        Ain't that good news!
    I've got a crown up in the Kingdom,
        Ain't that good news!

        Refrain:

        I'm a-goin' to lay down this world,
        Goin' to shoulder up my cross,
        Goin' to take it home to Jesus,
            Ain't that good news!

2. I've got a harp up in the Kingdom,
        (etc.)

3. I've got a robe up in the Kingdom,
        (etc.)

4. I've slippers in the Kingdom,
   (etc.)

5. I've a Savior in the Kingdom,
   (etc.)

Ain't That Good News!
(2nd version)

Ain't that good news,
Ain't that good news,
Ain't that good news,
   Oh, Lord!

Ain't that good news?

I'm going down to Jordan,
And I don't know for how long;
It's a life-time journey
But I'll soon get there.

The Bible says one thing,
I say the same,
Son of God drawing water,
Out of every vein.

God done made this religion
For to praise His holy name;
The clouds are hanging heavy,
That's sure a sign of rain.

One of these mornings,
And it won't be long,
I'll go away to heaven,
And I'm going in the storm.

A Little Talk with Jesus Makes It Right

O, a little talk with Jesus makes it right, all right;
Little talk with Jesus makes it right, all right.
   Lord, troubles of every kind,
   Thank God, I'll always find
That a little talk with Jesus makes it right.

My brother, I remember when I was a sinner lost,
I cried, "Have mercy, Jesus," but still my soul was tossed;
   Till I heard King Jesus say,
   "Come here, I am the way,"
And a little talk with Jesus makes it right.

Sometimes the forked lightning, and muttering thunder, too,
Of trials and temptation make it hard for me and you;
    But Jesus is our friend,
    He'll keep up till the end,
And a little talk with Jesus makes it right,
O, a little talk with Jesus makes it right.

    Lord, troubles of every kind,
    Thank God, I'll always find
That a little talk with Jesus makes it right.

All I Do, the Church Keep a-Grumbling

Refrain:

All I do, the church keep a-grumbling,
All I do, Lord, all I do;
All I do, the church keep a-grumbling,
All I do, Lord, all I do.

1. Try my best to serve my Master,
   Try my best to serve my Lord,
   Try my best to serve my Master,
      Hallelujah!

2. Try my best to follow the Leader,
   Try my best to serve my Lord,
   Try my best to follow my Leader,
      Hallelujah!

3. Kneel and pray so the devil won't harm me,
   Try my best to serve my Lord,
   Kneel and pray so the devil won't harm me,
      Hallelujah!

4. I'm going to cling to the ship of Zion,
   Try my best to serve my Lord,
   I'm going to cling to the ship of Zion,
      Hallelujah!

    All I do, the church keep a-grumbling,
    All I do, Lord, all I do;
    All I do, the church keep a-grumbling,
    All I do, Lord, all I do.

All Night, All Day

Refrain:

All night, all day,
Angels watchin' over me, my Lord;
All night, all day,
Angels watchin' over me.

1. Now I lay me down to sleep,
    Angels watchin' over me, my Lord,
    Pray the Lord my soul to keep,
    Angels watchin' over me.

    [*to Refrain*]

2. If I die before I wake,
    Angels watchin' over me, my Lord,
    Pray the Lord my soul to take.
    Angels watchin' over me.

    [*to Refrain*]

Anyhow, My Lord

Anyhow, anyhow, anyhow, my Lord,
At the cross you must bow;
I'm going to heaven, anyhow.

If your father talk about you,
And scandalize your name,
    At the cross you must bow,
    I'm going to heaven, anyhow.

If your mother talk about you,
And scandalize your name—
If your brother talk about you,
And scandalize your name—
If your sister talk about you,
And scandalize your name,
    At the cross you must bow,
    I'm going to heaven, anyhow.

Balm in Gilead
[There Is a Balm in Gilead]

Refrain:

There is a Balm in Gilead
To make the wounded whole,
There is a Balm in Gilead
To heal the sin-sick soul.

1. Sometimes I feel discouraged
   And think my work's in vain,
   But then the Holy Spirit
   Revives my soul again.

   [*to Refrain*]

2. Don't ever feel discouraged,
   For Jesus is your friend;
   And if you lack for knowledge,
   He'll ne'er refuse to lend.

   [*to Refrain*]

3. If you cannot sing like Peter,
   If you cannot preach like Paul,
   You can tell the love of Jesus
   And say, "He died for all."

   [*to Refrain*]

By and By

Refrain:

O, by and by, by and by,
I'm going to lay down my heavy load;
O, by and by, by and by,
I'm going to lay down my heavy load.

1. I know my robe's going to fit me well,
   I'm going to lay down my heavy load
   I tried it on at the gates of hell,
   I'm going to lay down my heavy load.

   [*to Refrain*]

2. Hell is deep and dark despair,
   I'm going to lay down my heavy load
   Stop, poor sinner, and don't go there,
   I'm going to lay down my heavy load.

   [*to Refrain*]

3. O, Christians, can't you rise and tell
   I'm going to lay down my heavy load
   That Jesus hath done all things well,
   I'm going to lay down my heavy load.

   [*to Refrain*]

Calvary

Refrain:

Calvary, Calvary,
Calvary, Calvary,
Calvary, Calvary,
Surely He died on Calvary.

1. Every time I think about Jesus,
   Every time I think about Jesus,
   Every time I think about Jesus,
   Surely He died on Calvary.

   [*to Refrain*]

2. Sinner, do you love my Jesus?
   Sinner, do you love my Jesus?
   Sinner, do you love my Jesus?
   Surely He died on Calvary.

   [*to Refrain*]

3. Makes me troubled thinking about dying,
   (*etc.*)

4. We are climbing Jacob's ladder,
   (*etc.*)

5. Every round goes higher and higher,
   (*etc.*)

Can't You Live Humble?

Can't you live humble?
Praise King Jesus!
Can't you live humble
To the dying Lamb?
Lightning flashes, thunders roll,
Make me think of my poor soul.
Come here, Jesus, come here, please,
See my Jesus, on my knees.

Everybody come and see,
A man's been here from Galilee.
Came down here, and he talked to me,
Went away and he left me free.
Can't you live humble?
Praise King Jesus!
Can't you live humble
To the dying Lamb?

Certainly, Lord

Leader & Chorus:

Have you got good religion?
Certainly, Lord.

Do you love everybody?
Certainly, Lord.

Have you been baptized?
Certainly, Lord.

Did your soul feel happy?
Certainly, Lord.

Have you been redeemed?
Certainly, Lord.

Did you run tell your sister?
Did you run tell your brother?
Did you run tell your mother?
Certainly, Lord.

Did you feel like shouting?
Certainly, Lord.

Chilly Water

Chilly water, chilly water,
Hallelujah to that Lamb, to that Lamb.

I know that water is chilly and cold,
But I have Jesus in my soul;

O, in that ark the little dove moaned,
Christ Jesus standing as the corner stone;

Old Satan's just like a snake in the grass,
He's watching to bite you as you pass;

O, brothers and sisters, come one and all,
You'd better be ready when the roll is called.

Hallelujah to that Lamb, to that Lamb,
Chilly water, chilly water,
Hallelujah to that Lamb, to that Lamb.

City Called Heaven

I am a poor pilgrim of sorrow,
I'm in this wide world along;
No hope in this world for tomorrow,
I'm trying to make heaven my home.

Sometimes I am tossed and driven,
Sometimes I don't know where to roam;
I've heard of a city called Heaven,
I've started to make it my home.

My mother's gone on to pure glory,
My father's still walking in sin;
My sisters and brothers won't own me
Because I'm trying to get in.

Sometimes I am tossed and driven,
Sometimes I don't know where to roam;
But I've heard of a city called Heaven,
And I've started to make it my home.

Come Here, Lord!

Come here, Lord!
Come here, Lord!
Sinner cryin', Come here, Lord!

O, little did I think He was so nigh,
Sinner cryin', Come here, Lord!
He spoke and made me laugh and cry.
Sinner cryin', Come here, Lord!

O, mourners, if you will believe,
Sinner cryin', Come here, Lord!
The grace of God you will receive.
Sinner cryin', Come here, Lord!

Some seek God's face, but don't seek right,
Sinner cryin', Come here, Lord!
They pray a little by day and none by night.
Sinner cryin', Come here, Lord!

O, sinner, you had better pray,
Sinner cryin', Come here, Lord!
For Satan's 'round you every day.
Sinner cryin', Come here, Lord!

Come here, Lord!
Come here, Lord!
Sinner cryin', Come here, Lord!

9

Daniel, Daniel, Servant of the Lord

Oh, the king cried,
Oh, Daniel, Daniel, oh!
Daniel, Daniel, oh!
A-that-a Hebrew Daniel,
A-that-a Hebrew Daniel,
Daniel, Daniel, oh!
Oh, Daniel, Daniel,
Servant of the Lord!

Among the Hebrew nation,
One Hebrew, Daniel, was found;
They put him in the lion's den,
He stayed there all night long.

Now, the king in his sleep was troubled,
And early in the morning he rose
To find God had sent his angel down
To lock the lion's jaws!

Oh, the king cried,
Oh, Daniel, Daniel, oh!
Servant of the Lord!

Deep River

Deep river,
My home is over Jordan;
Deep river, Lord,
I want to cross over into campground.

O, don't you want to go over to that gospel feast,
To that promised land where all is peace?

O, deep river,
My home is over Jordan;
Deep river, Lord,
I want to cross over into campground.

Didn't My Lord Deliver Daniel

Refrain:

Didn't my Lord deliver Daniel,
Didn't my Lord deliver Daniel,
Didn't my Lord deliver Daniel,
And why not every man?

1. He delivered Daniel from the lion's den,
   And Jonah from the belly of the whale,
   And the Hebrew children from the fiery furnace,
   And why not every man?

10

[*to Refrain*]

2. The moon run down in a purple stream,
   The sun forebear to shine;
   Every star disappear,
   King Jesus shall be mine.

   [*to Refrain*]

3. The wind blows east and the wind blows west,
   It blows like the Judgment Day;
   Every soul that never did pray
   Will be glad to pray that day.

   [*to Refrain*]

4. I will set my foot on the Gospel ship,
   And the ship it begin to sail;
   It landed me over on Canaan shore,
   I'll never come back anymore.

   [*to Refrain*]

Didn't Old Pharaoh Get Lost?

1. Isaac, a ransom,
   While he lay upon an altar bound;
   Moses, an infant cast away,
   By Pharaoh's daughter found;
   Joseph, by his false brethren sold,
   God raised above them all;
   To Hannah's child the Lord foretold
   How Eli's house should fail.

   Refrain:

   Didn't old Pharaoh get lost, get lost,
   Didn't old Pharaoh get lost, get lost
   In the Red Sea,
   True believer?

2. The Lord said unto Moses,
   "Go into Pharaoh now,
   For I have hardened Pharaoh's heart,
   To me he will not bow."
   Then Moses and Aaron
   To Pharaoh did go:
   "Thus says the God of Israel—
   Let my people go."

   [*to Refrain*]

3. Old Pharaoh said, "Who is the Lord
      That I should him obey?"
   "His name it is Jehovah,
      For he hears his people pray."
   Hark! Hear the children murmur,
      They cry aloud for bread;
   Down came the hidden manna,
      The hungry soldiers fed.

   [to Refrain]

4. Then Moses numbered Israel
      Through all the land abroad,
   Saying, "Children, do not murmur,
      But hear the word of God."
   Then Moses said to Israel
      As they stood along the shore,
   "Your enemies you see today,
      You'll never see no more."

   [to Refrain]

5. Then down came raging Pharaoh,
      That you may plainly see,
   Old Pharaoh and his host
      Got lost in the Red Sea.
   Then men and women and children
      To Moses they did flock;
   They cried aloud for water
      And Moses smote the rock.

   [to Refrain]

6. And the Lord spoke to Moses
      From Sinai's smoking top,
   Saying, "Moses, lead the people
      Till I shall bid you to stop."

      Didn't old Pharaoh get lost, get lost,
      Didn't old Pharaoh get lost, get lost
      In the Red Sea,
      True believer?

Do Lord, Remember Me

1. Do Lord, do Lord, do remember me,
   Do Lord, do Lord, do remember me,
   Do Lord, do Lord, do remember me,
   O, do Lord, remember me.

2. When I'm in trouble, do remember me,
   When I'm in trouble, do remember me,
   When I'm in trouble, do remember me,
   O, do Lord, remember me.

3. When I'm dyin', do remember me,
   When I'm dyin', do remember me,
   When I'm dyin', do remember me,
   O, do Lord, remember me.

4. When this world's on fire, do remember me,
   When this world's on fire, do remember me,
   When this world's on fire, do remember me,
   O, do Lord, remember me.

Done Found My Lost Sheep

Done found my lost sheep,
Done found my lost sheep,
Done found my lost sheep,
Hallelujah!

My Lord had a hundred sheep;
One of them did go astray.
That just left him ninety-nine
To go to the wilderness to seek and find.

If you find him, bring him back,
'Cross the shoulders across your back.
Tell the neighbors all around
That lost sheep has done been found.

In that Resurrection Day,
Sinner can't find no hiding place.
Go to the mountain, the mountain moves;
Run to the hill, the hill runs, too.

Sinner man traveling on trembling ground,
Poor lost sheep ain't ever been found.
Sinner, why don't you stop and pray,
Then you'd hear the Shepherd say:

Done found my lost sheep,
Done found my lost sheep,
Done found my lost sheep,
Hallelujah!

Don't Be Weary, Traveller

Don't be weary, traveller, traveller,
Come along home to Jesus;
Don't be weary, traveller, traveller,
Come along home to Jesus.

My head got wet with the midnight dew,
Angels bear me witness, too;

Where to go, I did not know
Ever since He freed my soul;
    I look at the world and the world looks new,
    I look at the world and the world looks new.

Don't be weary, traveller, traveller,
Come along home to Jesus;
Don't be weary, traveller, traveller,
Come along home to Jesus.

Upon the mountain my Lord spoke,
Out of his mouth came fire and smoke;
    All around me looks so fine,
    Asked my Lord if all was mine;
        Jordan river is chilly and cold,
        Chills the body but not the soul.

Every time I feel the Spring moving in my heart,
    I will pray.
Every time I feel the Spring moving in my heart,
    I will pray.

Don't be weary, traveller, traveller,
Come along home to Jesus;
Don't be weary, traveller, traveller,
Come along home to Jesus.

Down by the Riverside

1. Gonna lay down my sword and shield
    Down by the riverside
    Down by the riverside
    Down by the riverside
    Gonna lay down my sword and shield
    Down by the riverside
    And study war no more.

    Refrain:
    Ain't gonna study war no more,
    Ain't gonna study war no more,
    Ain't gonna study war no more,

2. Gonna put on my long white robe
    Down by the riverside
    Down by the riverside
    Down by the riverside
    Gonna put on my long white robe
    Down by the riverside
    And study war no more.

    [*to Refrain*]

3. Gonna talk with the Prince of Peace
   (etc.)

4. Gonna join hands with everyone
   (etc.)

Dry Bones Gonna Rise Again

All them bones, all them bones,
In the morning, all them bones,
Dry bones gonna rise again.

Some of them bones, my mother's bones;
Some of them bones, my father's bones.
Dry bones gonna rise again.

Sinners go to meeting house to sing and shout,
By the preacher surely will turn them out.
Dry bones gonna rise again.

If you want to get a seat in heaven on high,
Don't you steal, don't you 'dulter, and don't you lie.
Dry bones gonna rise again.

Got my religion and I got it good and strong,
'Cause God Almighty never done me wrong.
Dry bones gonna rise again.

God called Ezekiel by His Word:
"Go down and prophesy!"
    "Yes, Lord!"

Ezekiel prophesied by the power of God,
Commanded the bones to rise:
    "Dry bones, they gonna walk around,
    Dry bones, they gonna walk around,
    Dry bones, why don't you rise
        and hear the Word of the Lord!"

("Tell me, how did the bones get together
        with the leg bone? Prophesy!")

Chorus:
Ah well:
The toe bone connected with the foot bone;
The foot bone connected with the ankle bone;
The ankle bone connected with the leg bone;
The leg bone connected with the knee bone;
The knee bone connected with the thigh bone;
    Rise and hear the Word of the Lord!

Elijah, Rock!

Elijah, rock!
　　Shout! Shout!
Elijah, rock!
　　Shout! Shout!
Elijah, rock!
　　Calling up the Lord.

　　(repeat)

Elijah! ——
Elijah! ——

Elijah, rock!
　　Shout! Shout!
Elijah, rock!
　　Shout! Shout!
Elijah, rock!
　　Calling up the Lord.

Every Time I Feel the Spirit

Every time I feel the spirit
　　moving in my heart,
　　　　I will pray;
Every time I feel the spirit
　　moving in my heart,
　　　　I will pray.

Upon the mountain my Lord spoke,
Out of His mouth came fire and smoke;
　　All around me looks so fine,
　　Asked my Lord if all was mine;
　　　　Jordan river is chilly and cold,
　　　　Chills the body but not the soul.

Every time I feel the spirit
　　moving in my heart,
　　　　I will pray;
Every time I feel the spirit
　　moving in my heart,
　　　　I will pray.

Ezekiel Saw the Wheel

　　Refrain:

　　Ezekiel saw the wheel
　　　　'Way up in the middle of the air,
　　Ezekiel saw the wheel
　　　　'Way up in the middle of the air.

The big wheel moved by faith,
Little wheel moved by the Grace of God:
A wheel in a wheel
'Way up in the middle of the air.

1. Just let me tell you what a hypocrite'll do:
   'Way up in the middle of the air,
   He'll talk about me and he'll talk about you!
   'Way up in the middle of the air.

2. Watch out, my sister, how you walk on the cross,
   'Way up in the middle of the air,
   Your foot might slip, and your soul get lost!
   'Way up in the middle of the air.

3. You say the Lord has set you free?
   'Way up in the middle of the air,
   Why don't you let your neighbor be!
   'Way up in the middle of the air.

4. Ezekiel saw the wheel
   'Way up in the middle of the air,
   And every spoke was humankind!
   'Way up in the middle of the air.

   [*to Refrain*]

Fare Ye Well

O, fare ye well, my brother,
Fare ye well by the grace of God,
For I'm going home.
    I'm going home, my Lord,
    I'm going home.

Master Jesus gave me a little broom
To sweep my heart clean;
Sweep it clean by the grace of God,
And glory in my soul.

Fix Me, Jesus

Oh, fix me, Jesus, fix me right,
Fix me right, fix me right;
Oh, fix me, Jesus, fix me right,
Fix me so I can stand.

Oh, place my feet on solid ground,
Oh, place my feet on solid ground;
Oh, when I die, you must bury me deep,
Oh, when I die, you must bury me deep.

Oh, dig my grave with a silver spade,
Oh, dig my grave with a silver spade;
And let me down with a golden chain,
And let me down with a golden chain.

Oh, fix me, Jesus, fix me right,
Fix me right, fix me right;
Oh, fix me, Jesus, fix me right,
Fix me so I can stand.

Free at Last

(1st version)

Refrain:

Free at last, free at last,
Thank God Almighty, I'm free at last;
Free at last, free at last,
Thank God Almighty, I'm free at last.

O, remember the day,
I remember it well;
My dungeon shook
And my chain fell off.

[to Refrain]

I know my Lord is a man of war,
He fought my battle at hell's dark door;
Satan thought he had me fast,
I broke his chain and got free at last.
Satan's mad and I'm glad,
I hope to God to keep him mad.

[to Refrain]

You can hinder me here, but you can't hinder me there,
The Lord in heaven's gonna answer my prayer.
I went in the valley, but I didn't go to stay,
My soul got happy and I stayed all day.
O, this ain't all, I got more besides—
I'm born of God and I've been baptized.

[to Refrain]

Free at Last

(2nd version)

Refrain:

Free at last, free at last,
I thank God, I'm free at last!
Free at last, free at last,
I thank God, I'm free at last!

1. 'Way down yonder, in the graveyard walk,
   I thank God, I'm free at last,
   Me and my Jesus going to meet and talk.
   I thank God, I'm free at last!

   [*to Refrain*]

2. On my knees when the light passed by,
   I thank God, I'm free at last,
   Thought my soul would rise and fly.
   I thank God, I'm free at last!

   [*to Refrain*]

3. Some of these mornings, bright and fair,
   I thank God, I'm free at last,
   Going to meet King Jesus in the air.
   I thank God, I'm free at last!

   [*to Refrain*]

Give Me Jesus

1. I heard my mother say,
   I heard my mother say,
   I heard my mother say,
     "Give me Jesus."

   Refrain:

   Give me Jesus,
   Give me Jesus;
   You may have all the world,
   Give me Jesus.

2. [At] dark midnight, was my cry,
   Dark midnight, was my cry,
   Dark midnight, was my cry,
     "Give me Jesus."

   [*to Refrain*]

3. In the morning when I rise,
     (*etc.*)

   [*to Refrain*]

4. And when I come to die,
     (*etc.*)

   [*to Refrain*]

5. I heard the mourner say,
   I heard the mourner say,
   "You may have all the world,
     Give me Jesus,
     Give me Jesus."

   [*to Refrain*]

19

Give Me That Old-Time Religion

Refrain:

Give me that old-time religion,
Give me that old-time religion,
Give me that old-time religion,
It's good enough for me.

1. It was good for our mothers,
   It was good for our mothers,
   It was good for our mothers,
   And it's good enough for me.

   [*to Refrain*]

2. It was good for our fathers,
   (etc.)

3. It was good for the Prophet Daniel,
   (etc.)

4. It was good for the Hebrew children,
   (etc.)

5. It was tried in the fiery furnace,
   (etc.)

6. It was good for Paul and Silas,
   (etc.)

7. It will do when the world's on fire,
   (etc.)

8. It will do when I'm dying,
   (etc.)

9. It will take us all to heaven,
   (etc.)

10. Makes me love everybody,
    (etc.)

Give Me Your Hand

Refrain:

O, give me your hand, give me your hand,
All I want is the love of God;
Give me your hand, give me your hand,
You must be loving at God's command.

1. You say you're aiming at the skies,
    You must be loving at God's command,
   Why don't you quit your telling lies?
    You must be loving at God's command.

   [*to Refrain*]

2. You say the Lord has set you free,
    You must be loving at God's command,
   Why don't you let your neighbor be?
    You must be loving at God's command.

   [*to Refrain*]

3. Some seek God's face, but don't seek right,
    You must be loving at God's command,
   Pray in the day, but none at night,
    You must be loving at God's command.

   [*to Refrain*]

God Is a God!

God is a God!
God don't never change!
God is a God,
And He always will be God!

He made the sun to shine by day,
He made the sun to show the way,
He made the stars to show their light,
He made the moon to shine by night,
    saying—

God is a God!
God don't never change!
God is a God,
And He always will be God!

The Earth's His footstool and heaven's His throne;
The whole creation, all His own;
His love and power will prevail,
His promises will never fail,
    saying—

God is a God!
God don't never change!
God is a God,
And He always will be God!

Go Down, Moses

[Let My People Go] [Down in Egypt's Land]

1. When Israel was in Egypt's land,
   Let my people go,
   Oppressed so hard they could not stand.
   Let my people go.
   Go down, Moses, 'way down in Egypt's land,
   Tell ol' Pharaoh, let my people go.

2. "Thus saith the Lord," bold Moses said,
   Let my people go,
   "If not, I'll smite your first-born dead!"
   Let my people go.
   Go down, Moses, 'way down in Egypt's land,
   Tell ol' Pharaoh, let my people go.

3. No more shall they in bondage toil,
   Let my people go,
   Let them come out with Egypt's spoil.
   Let my people go.
   Go down, Moses, 'way down in Egypt's land,
   Tell ol' Pharaoh, let my people go.

   [Verses 4–11 continue in the same pattern]

4. The Lord told Moses what to do
   To lead his people right on through.

5. 'Twas on a dark and dismal night
   When Moses led the Israelites.

6. "Oh, Moses, clouds will cleave the way,
   A fire by night, a shade by day."

7. When Israel reached the water side,
   Commanded God, "It shall divide."

8. "Come, Moses, you will not get lost.
   Stretch out your rod and come across."

9. When they had reached the other shore,
   They sang a song of triumph o'er.

10. Now Pharaoh said he'd go across,
    But Pharaoh and his host were lost.

11. Oh, take your shoes from off your feet
    And walk into the golden street.

Going Home in the Chariot

Refrain:

Going home in the chariot in the morning,
Going home in the chariot in the morning,
Going home in the chariot in the morning,
Going home in the chariot in the morning.

1. O, never you mind what Satan say,
       Going home in the chariot in the morning,
    He never did teach one sinner to pray,
       Going home in the chariot in the morning.

    [*to Refrain*]

2. O, sinner-man, you better pray,
       Going home in the chariot in the morning,
    For judgment is coming every day,
       Going home in the chariot in the morning.

    [*to Refrain*]

3. O, mourner, mourner, you must believe,
       Going home in the chariot in the morning,
    And the grace of God you will receive,
       Going home in the chariot in the morning.

    [*to Refrain*]

Going to Heaven

The Book of Revelation God to us revealed
Mysteries of salvation, The Book of Seven Seals.
    Going to heaven,
    Going to heaven,
Going to heaven to see that bleeding Lamb.

John saw the heavens open, the Conqueror riding down;
He looked and saw white horses and rider following on.

If you want to know the Conqueror, He is the Word of God,
His eyes are like a burning throne, He is the Word of God.

Hosanna! to the Prince of Life, who clothes Himself in clay,
And entered the iron gate of death and bore the ties away.

See how the Conqueror mounts aloft and to His Father flies
With scars of honor on His flesh and trials in His eyes.

The Book of Revelation God to us revealed
Mysteries of salvation, The Book of Seven Seals.
    Going to heaven,
    Going to heaven,
Going to heaven to see that bleeding Lamb.

Going to Sing All Along the Way

O, I'm going to sing, going to sing,
Going to sing all along the way;
O, I'm going to sing, going to sing,
Going to sing all along the way.

We'll raise the Christians' banner,
The motto new and old:
Repentance and salvation
Are engravéd there in gold.

We'll shout over all our sorrows,
And sing forevermore
With Christ and all his army
On that celestial shore.

O, I'm going to sing, going to sing,
Going to sing all along the way;
O, I'm going to sing, going to sing,
Going to sing all along the way.

Going Up to Glory

Refrain:

O, yes, I'm going up, going up,
  Going all the way, Lord;
Going up, going up,
  To see the heavenly land.
O, saints and sinners, will you go
  See the heavenly land?
I'm going up to heaven for to see my robe,
  See the heavenly land;
Going to see my robe and try it on,
  See the heavenly land;
It's brighter than that glittering sun,
  See the heavenly land.

I'm going to keep a-climbing high
Till I meet those angels in the sky,
Those pretty angels I shall see—
Why don't the Devil let me be?

[*to Refrain*]

I tell you what I like the best:
It is them shouting Methodists;
We shout so loud then Devil looks
And he gets away with his cloven foot.

[*to Refrain*]

24

Gonna Shout All Over God's Heaven

[Heaven]

1. I've got a robe, you've got a robe,
   All of God's children got a robe;
   When I get to heaven, gonna put on my robe,
   Gonna shout all over God's heaven.

   Refrain:
   Heaven, heaven,
   Everybody talking 'bout heaven
      ain't going there,
   Heaven, heaven,
   Gonna shout all over God's heaven.

2. I've got a crown, you've got a crown,
   All of God's children got a crown;
   When I get to heaven, gonna put on my crown,
   Gonna shout all over God's heaven.

   [*to Refrain*]

3. I've got shoes, you've got shoes,
   All of God's children got shoes;
   When I get to heaven, gonna put on my shoes,
   Gonna walk all over God's heaven.

   [*to Refrain*]

4. I've got a harp, you've got a harp,
   All of God's children got a harp;
   When I get to heaven, gonna play on my harp,
   Gonna play all over God's heaven.

   [*to Refrain*]

5. I've got a song, you've got a song,
   All of God's children got a song;
   When I get to heaven, gonna sing my new song,
   Gonna sing all over God's heaven.

   [*to Refrain*]

Good Lord, I Done Done

Good Lord, I done done,
Good Lord, I done done,
Good Lord, I done done,
I done done what you told me to do.

Leader & Chorus:

You told me to pray, and I done that, too;
   I done done what you told me to do.
I prayed and prayed till I come through;
   I done done what you told me to do.

25

You told me to mourn, and I done that, too;
  I done done what you told me to do.
I mourned and I mourned till I come through;
  I done done what you told me to do.

You told me to shout, and I done that, too;
  I done done what you told me to do.
I shout and I shout till I come through;
  I done done what you told me to do.

  Good Lord, I done done,
  Good Lord, I done done,
  Good Lord, I done done,
  I done done what you told me to do.

Good News!
(1st version)

Good news! Good news!
Angel bring glad tidings down!
Good news! Good news!
I hear from heaven today!

My brother have a robe and I so glad.
  Good news! Good news!
My brother have a robe and I so glad.
  Good news from heaven today!

O, heaven so high and so low,
  Good news! Good news!
I wonder in my soul if I ever get there.
  Good news from heaven today!

Good news! Good news!
Angel bring glad tidings down!
Good news! Good news!
I hear from heaven today!

Good News!
(2nd version)

  Refrain:

    Good news, the chariot's coming,
    Good news, the chariot's coming,
    Good news, the chariot's coming,
    And I don't want it to leave me behind.

1. There's a long, white robe in the heaven I know,
    There's a long, white robe in the heaven I know,
    There's a long, white robe in the heaven I know,
      And I don't want it to leave me behind.

26

[to Refrain]

2. There's a brand new song in the heaven I know,
There's a brand new song in the heaven I know,
There's a brand new song in the heaven I know,
    And I don't want it to leave me behind.

   [to Refrain]

Gospel Train

The gospel train is coming through,
The sun is getting out of view;
And if you get there before I do,
Tell them I'm coming by and by.

Stars in the heaven number one, number two,
Number three, number four,
Good Lord, good Lord,
Good Lord, by and by.

There was a camp meeting 'way down in the swamp,
    O, Lord, hallelujah!
Got so dark they had to get a lamp.
    O, Lord, hallelujah!

The preacher he was long and the preacher he was loud,
    O, Lord, hallelujah!
Along came an alligator and scared away the crowd.
    O, Lord, hallelujah!

Said the blackbird to the crow,
    O, Lord, hallelujah!
"What makes the farmer hate us so?"
    O, Lord, hallelujah!

Ever since Adam and Eve were made,
    O, Lord, hallelujah!
Pulling up the corn is just our trade.
    O, Lord, hallelujah!

The gospel train is coming through,
The sun is getting out of view;
And if you get there before I do,
Tell them I'm coming by and by.

Great Day!

Great day! Great day, the righteous marching.
Great day! God's going to build up Zion's walls!

1. Chariot rode on the mountain top,
    God's going to build up Zion's walls!
    My God spoke and the chariot did stop.
    God's going to build up Zion's walls!

2. This is the day of Jubilee,
    God's going to build up Zion's walls!
    The Lord has set His people free.
    God's going to build up Zion's walls!

3. We want no cowards in our band,
    God's going to build up Zion's walls!
    We call for valiant-hearted men.
    God's going to build up Zion's walls!

4. Gonna take my breast-plate, sword and shield,
    God's going to build up Zion's walls!
    And march out boldly in the field.
    God's going to build up Zion's walls!

Great day! Great day, the righteous marching.
Great day! God's going to build up Zion's walls!

Hallelujah!

Hallelujah! Hallelujah!
I do belong to the band, hallelu!

I have a sister, in that day
She'll take wings and fly away.
    I do belong to the band, hallelu!

I never shall forget that day
When Jesus washed my sins away.
    I do belong to the band, hallelu!

Looked at my hands and my hands looked new;
Looked at my feet and they looked so, too.
    I do belong to the band, hallelu!

I never felt such love before,
Saying, "Go in peace and sin no more."
    I do belong to the band, hallelu!

Hard Trials

The foxes have holes in the ground,
The birds have nests in the air,
The Christians have a hiding place,
But we poor sinners have none.
Now ain't them hard trials, tribulations?
Ain't them hard trials?
I'm going to live with God!

1. Old Satan tempted Eve,
   And Eve, she tempted Adam;
   And that's why the sinner has to pray so hard
   To get his sins forgiven.

2. Oh, Methodist, Methodist is my name,
   Methodist till I die;
   I'll be baptized on the Methodist side,
   And a Methodist will I die.

3. Oh, Baptist, Baptist is my name
   Baptist till I die;
   I'll be baptized on the Baptist side,
   And a Baptist will I die,

4. While marching on the road,
   A-hunting for a home,
   You had better stop your differences
   And travel on to God.

   The foxes have holes in the ground,
   The birds have nests in the air,
   The Christians have a hiding place,
   But we poor sinners have none.
   Now ain't them hard trials, tribulations?
   Ain't them hard trials?
   I'm going to live with God!

Heaven-Bound Soldier

Hold out your light,
        You heaven-bound soldier,
Hold out your light,
        You heaven-bound soldier,
Hold out your light,
        You heaven-bound soldier,
Let your light shine around the world.

O, deacon, can't you hold out your light,
O, preacher, can't you hold out your light,
Let your light shine around the world.

Heaven, Sweet Heaven

Heaven, sweet heaven,
Oh Lord, I want to go to heaven;
Heaven, sweet heaven,
Oh Lord, I want to go to heaven.

You lie on me,
They lie on you,
Lie on everybody;
The last lie you told on me,
It's going to raise me higher in heaven.

Ezekiel saw the mighty big wheel,
In the big wheel there was a little wheel,
The big wheel represents God Himself,
And the little wheel represents Jesus Christ.

He Is King of Kings

He is King of Kings.
He is Lord of Lords.
Jesus Christ, the first and last,
No man works like Him.

He built His throne up in the air,
No man works like Him.
And called His saints from everywhere.
No man works like Him.

He pitched His tents on Canaan's ground,
No man works like Him.
And broke the Roman kingdom down.
No man works like Him.

I know that my redeemer lives,
No man works like Him.
And by His death, sweet blessings gives.
No man works like Him.

He is King of Kings.
He is Lord of Lords.
Jesus Christ, the first and last,
No man works like Him.

He Never Said a Mumblin' Word

1. They led Him to Pilate's bar,
    Not a word, not a word, not a word, not a word,
   They led Him to Pilate's bar,
    Not a word, not a word, not a word, not a word,
   They led Him to Pilate's bar,
   But He never said a mumblin' word—
    Not a word, not a word, not a word, not a word.

2. They all cried, "Crucify Him!"
    Not a word, not a word, not a word, not a word,
   They all cried, "Crucify Him!"
    Not a word, not a word, not a word, not a word,
   They all cried, "Crucify Him!"
   But He never said a mumblin' word—
    Not a word, not a word, not a word, not a word.

3. They nailed Him to the tree,
    (etc.)

4. They pierced Him in the side,
    (etc.)

5. He hung His head and died,
    (etc.)

6. They laid Him in the tomb,
    (etc.)

7. Wasn't that a pity and a shame?
    (etc.)

He's Got His Eyes on You

He's got His eyes on you,
He's got His eyes on you,
My Lord's sitting in the Kingdom,
He's got His eyes on you.

I would not be a sinner,
I tell you the reason why:
'Fraid my Lord might call me,
And I wouldn't be ready to die.

I would not be a gambler,
I tell you the reason why:
'Fraid my Lord might call me,
And I wouldn't be ready to die.

I would not be a liar,
I tell you the reason why:
'Fraid my Lord might call me,
And I wouldn't be ready to die.

He's got His eyes on you,
He's got His eyes on you,
My Lord's sitting in the Kingdom,
He's got His eyes on you.

He's Got the Whole World in His Hand

He's got the whole world in His hand,
He's got the big, round world in His hand,
He's got the whole world in His hand,
He's got the whole world in His hand.

He's got the wind and the rain in His hand,
He's got the sun and moon in His hand,
He's got the wind and the rain in His hand,
He's got the whole world in His hand.

He's got the little bitsy baby in His hand,
He's got the tiny little baby in His hand,
He's got the little bitsy baby in His hand,
He's got the whole world in His hand.

He's got you and me, brother, in His hand,
He's got you and me, sister, in His hand,
He's got you and me, brother, in His hand,
He's got the whole world in His hand.

He's got everybody in His hand,
He's got everybody in His hand,
He's got everybody in His hand,
He's got the whole world in His hand.

Hold On!

Keep your hand on-a that plow!
Hold on!
Hold on! Hold on!
Keep your right hand on-a that plow!
Hold on!

Noah, let me come in,
Doors all fastened and the windows pinned.
Keep your right hand on-a that plow!
Noah said, You done lost your track,
Can't plow straight and keep-a lookin' back.

Sister Mary had a gold chain;
Every link was my Jesus' name.
Keep your hand on-a that plow!
Keep on plowin' and don't you tire;
Every row goes higher and higher.

If you want to get to Heaven
I'll tell you how:
Keep your right hand on-a that plow!
If that plow stays in-a your hand,
Land you straight in the Promised Land.

Humble Yourself, The Bell Done Rung

Live humble, humble, Lord;
Humble yourself, the bell done rung;
Live humble, humble, Lord;
Humble yourself, the bell done rung.
Glory and honor! Praise King Jesus!
Glory and honor! Praise the Lord!
Glory and honor! Praise King Jesus!
Glory and honor! Praise the Lord!

Oh, my young Christians, I got lots to tell you,
Jesus Christ speaking through the organs of the clay.
("One day, one day, Lord!")
God's going to call them children
        from a distant land.
Tombstones a-cracking, graves a-busting,
Hell and the sea are going to give up the dead.

False pretender wears sheep clothing on his back,
In his heart he's like a raving wolf.
("Judge ye not, my brothers!")
For ye shall be judged false pretender
        getting in the Christian band.

Watch that sun how steady he runs,
Don't let him catch you with your work undone.
Ever see such a man as God?

Hush, Hush, Somebody's Calling My Name
[Somebody's Calling My Name]

Hush, oh, hush,
Somebody's calling my name,
Hush, oh, hush,
Somebody's calling my name,
Hush, oh, hush,
Somebody's calling my name,

Oh, my Lord,
Oh, my Lord,
What shall I do?

I'm so glad
I got my religion in time,
I'm so glad
I got my religion in time,
Oh, my Lord,
Oh, my Lord,
What shall I do?

I Believe I'll Go Back Home

I believe I'll go back home
And acknowledge that I done wrong.

When I was in my Father's house,
I was well supplied.
I made a mistake in a-doin' well,
Now I'm dissatisfied.

Lordy, won't you help me in this field?

I believe I'll go back home
And acknowledge that I done wrong.

When I was in my Father's House,
I had bread enough to spare.
But now I'm sick and a-hungry too,
And ashamed to go back there.

Lordy, won't you help me in this field?

I believe I'll go back home.

I Couldn't Hear Nobody Pray

Chorus:

And I couldn't hear nobody pray,
And I couldn't hear nobody pray,
O, way down yonder by myself,
And I couldn't hear nobody pray.

Leader & Chorus:

In the valley!
　　I couldn't hear nobody pray,
On my knees!
　　I couldn't hear nobody pray,

With my burden!
    I couldn't hear nobody pray,
And my Saviour!
    I couldn't hear nobody pray,
O, Lord!—

    [*to Chorus*]

Leader & Chorus:

Chilly waters!
    [*responses as before*]
In the Jordan!
Crossing over!
Into Canaan!
O, Lord!—

    [*to Chorus*]

Hallelujah!
Troubles over!
In the kingdom!
With my Jesus!
O, Lord!—

    [*to Chorus*]

I Feel Like My Time Ain't Long

Refrain:

I feel like, I feel like, Lord,
I feel like my time ain't long;
I feel like, I feel like, Lord,
I feel like my time ain't long.

Went to the graveyard the other day,
    I feel like my time ain't long,
I looked at the place where my mother lay,
    I feel like my time ain't long.

Sometimes I'm up, and sometimes I'm down,
    I feel like my time ain't long,
And sometimes I'm almost on the ground,
    I feel like my time ain't long.

Mind out, my brother, how you walk on the cross,
    I feel like my time ain't long,
Your foot might slip and your soul get lost,
    I feel like my time ain't long.

I feel like, I feel like, Lord,
I feel like my time ain't long;
I feel like, I feel like, Lord,
I feel like my time ain't long.

I Got a Home in That Rock

1. I got a home in that Rock,
   Don't you see?
   I got a home in that Rock,
   Don't you see?

   Between the earth and the sky,
   'Though I heard my Saviour cry,
   You got a home in that Rock,
   Don't you see?

2. Poor man Lazarus, poor as I,
   Don't you see?
   Poor man Lazarus, poor as I,
   Don't you see?

   Poor man Lazarus, poor as I,
   When he died, he found a home on high;
   He had a home in that Rock,
   Don't you see?

3. Rich man Dives, he lived so well,
   Don't you see?
   Rich man Dives, he lived so well,
   Don't you see?

   Rich man Dives, he lived so well,
   When he died, he found a home in hell;
   He had not a home in that Rock,
   Don't you see?

4. God gave Noah the rainbow sign,
   Don't you see?
   God gave Noah the rainbow sign,
   Don't you see?

   God gave Noah the rainbow sign,
   No more water, but fire next time;
   Better get a home in that Rock,
   Don't you see?

I Know the Lord's Laid His Hands on Me

O, I know the Lord, I know the Lord,
I know the Lord's laid His hands on me!

Did you ever see the like before?
I know the Lord's laid His hands on me,
King Jesus preaching to the poor.
I know the Lord's laid His hands on me!

O, wasn't that a happy day
I know the Lord's laid His hands on me,
When Jesus washed my sins away!
I know the Lord's laid His hands on me!

Some seek the Lord and don't seek Him right,
I know the Lord's laid His hands on me,
They fool all day and trifle all night.
I know the Lord's laid His hands on me!

My Lord has done just what He said,
I know the Lord's laid His hands on me,
Healed the sick and raised the dead.
I know the Lord's laid His hands on me!

O, I know the Lord, I know the Lord,
I know the Lord's laid His hands on me!

I'm a-Rolling

I'm a-rolling, I'm a-rolling,
I'm a-rolling through an unfriendly world;
I'm a-rolling, I'm a-rolling,
I'm a-rolling through an unfriendly world.

O, brothers, won't you help me to pray?
O, sisters, won't you help me in the service of the Lord?

I'm a-rolling, I'm a-rolling,
I'm a-rolling through an unfriendly world;
I'm a-rolling, I'm a-rolling,
I'm a-rolling through an unfriendly world.

I'm a-Troubled in the Mind

I'm a-troubled in the mind,
O, I'm a-troubled in the mind;
I ask my Lord what shall I do?
I'm a-troubled in the mind.

I'm a-troubled in the mind,
O, I'm a-troubled in the mind;
What you doubt for?
I'm a-troubled in the mind.

I'm Going Up to Heaven, Anyhow

Anyhow, anyhow, anyhow, my Lord!
Anyhow, yes, anyhow;
I'm going up to heaven anyhow.

If your brother talks about you,
And scandalizes your name,
Down at the cross you must bow;
If your sister talks about you,
And scandalizes your name,
Down at the cross you must bow;
If your preacher talks about you,
And scandalizes your name,
Down at the cross you must bow;
If your deacon talks about you,
And scandalizes your name,
Down at the cross you must bow.

Anyhow, anyhow, anyhow, my Lord!
Anyhow, yes, anyhow;
I'm going up to heaven anyhow.

I'm Just Going Over There

I'm just going over Jordan,
I'm just going over there;
I'm going home to see my brother,
I'm just going over there.

I'm just going over Jordan,
I'm just going over there;
I'm going home to see my mother,
I'm just going over there.

I'm just going over Jordan,
I'm just going over there;
I'm going home to see my Jesus,
I'm just going over there.

In-a That Morning

You may bury me in the East,
You may bury me in the West,
But I'll hear the trumpet sound
In-a that morning!

In-a that morning, my Lord!
How I long to go
For to hear the trumpet sound
In-a that morning!

In That Great Getting-Up Morning

[*Leader*]

I'm gonna tell you about the coming of the Saviour,
Fare you well, fare you well.
I'm gonna tell you about the coming of the Saviour,
Fare you well, fare you well.

1. There's a better day a-coming,
     Fare you well, fare you well,
   O, preacher, fold your Bible;
     Fare you well, fare you well,
   Prayer-maker, pray no more,
     Fare you well, fare you well,
   For the last soul's converted.
     Fare you well, fare you well.

2. That the time shall be no longer,
     Fare you well, fare you well,
   For Judgment Day is coming;
     Fare you well, fare you well,
   Then you hear the sinner saying,
     Fare you well, fare you well,
   Down I'm rolling, down I'm rolling.
     Fare you well, fare you well.

   [*Leader*]

   In that great getting-up morning,
   Fare you well, fare you well,
   In that great getting-up morning,
   Fare you well, fare you well.

3. The Lord spoke to Gabriel,
     Fare you well, fare you well,
   "Go look behind the altar;
     Fare you well, fare you well,
   Take down the silver trumpet,
     Fare you well, fare you well,
   Bow your trumpet, Gabriel."
     Fare you well, fare you well.

   [*responses continue throughout*]

4. "Lord, how loud shall I blow it?"
     "Blow it right calm and easy;
   Do not alarm my people;
     Tell them to come to judgment."

5. "Gabriel, blow your trumpet."
     "Lord, how loud shall I blow it?"
   "Loud as seven peals of thunder—
     Wake the living nations."

39

6. Place one foot upon the dry land,
   Place the other on the sea,
   Then you'll see the coffins busting,
   See the dry bones come a-creeping.

7. Hell shall be uncapped and burning,
   Then the dragon shall be loosened!
   Where you running, poor sinner?
   Where you running, poor sinner?

   [*Leader*]

   In that great getting-up morning,
   Fare you well, fare you well,
   In that great getting-up morning,
   Fare you well, fare you well.

8. Then you'll see poor sinners rising,
   Then you'll see the world on fire;
   See the moon a-bleeding,
   See the stars a-falling;
   See the elements a-melting,
   See the forked lightning.

9. Then you'll cry out for cold water,
   While the Christians shout in glory:
   Saying Amen to your damnation,
   No mercy for poor sinner.

   [*Leader*]

   In that great getting-up morning,
   Fare you well, fare you well,
   In that great getting-up morning,
   Fare you well, fare you well.

10. Hear the rumbling of the thunder,
    Earth shall reel and totter;
    Then you'll see the Christian rising,
    Then you'll see the righteous marching.
    See them marching home to heaven.

11. Then you'll see my Jesus coming
    With all His holy angels,
    Take the righteous home to glory;
    There they live with God forever,
    On the right-hand side of my Saviour.

    [*Leader*]

    In that great getting-up morning,
    Fare you well, fare you well,
    In that great getting-up morning,
    Fare you well, fare you well.

In the Mansions Above

Good Lord, in the mansions above,
Good Lord, in the mansions above,
My Lord, I hope to meet my Jesus
In the mansions above.

If you get to heaven before I do,
Lord, tell my Jesus I'm a-coming too,
To the mansions above.

My Lord, I've had many crosses and tribulations
   here below;
My Lord, I hope to meet you
In the mansions above.

Fight on, my brother, for the mansions above,
For I hope to meet my Jesus there
In the mansions above.

Good Lord, in the mansions above,
Good Lord, in the mansions above,
My Lord, I hope to meet my Jesus
In the mansions above.

Is There Anybody Here?

Refrain:

Is there anybody here who loves my Jesus?
Anybody here who loves my Lord?
I want to know if you love my Jesus;
I want to know if you love my Lord.

This world's a wilderness of woe,
So let us all to glory go.

   [*to Refrain*]

Religion is a blooming rose,
And none but them who feel it know.

   [*to Refrain*]

When I was blind and could not see,
King Jesus brought the light to me.

   [*to Refrain*]

When every star refuse to shine,
I know King Jesus will be mine.

   [*to Refrain*]

41

It's Me, O Lord

It's me, it's me, it's me, O Lord,
Standing in the need of prayer;
It's me, it's me, it's me, O Lord,
Standing in the need of prayer.

'T'ain't my mother or my father,
But it's me, O Lord,
Standing in the need of prayer.

'T'ain't my deacon or my leader,
But it's me, O Lord,
Standing in the need of prayer.

I've Been 'Buked

I've been 'buked and I've been scorned,
  O, Lord—
I've been 'buked and I've been scorned,
  Children—
I've been 'buked and I've been scorned,
I've been talked about sure's you're born.

But, ain't goin' to lay my 'ligion down,
  No, Lord—
Ain't goin' to lay my 'ligion down,
  Children—
No, ain't goin' to lay my 'ligion down,
Ain't goin' to lay my 'ligion down.

I've Been in the Storm So Long

Refrain:

  I've been in the storm so long,
  I've been in the storm so long, children;
  I've been in the storm so long,
  O, give me little time to pray.

1. O, let me tell my mother how I come along,
    O, give me little time to pray,
  With a hung-down head and aching heart.
    O, give me little time to pray.

2. O, when I got to heaven, I'll walk all about,
    O, give me little time to pray,
  There'll be nobody there to turn me out.
    O, give me little time to pray.

  [*to Refrain*]

I Want to Be Ready

Refrain:

I want to be ready, I want to be ready,
I want to be ready to walk in Jerusalem just like John.

1. O, John, O John, what do you say?
   Walk in Jerusalem just like John,
   That I'll be there at the coming day.
   Walk in Jerusalem just like John.

2. John said the city was just four-square,
   Walk in Jerusalem just like John,
   And he declared he'd meet me there.
   Walk in Jerusalem just like John.

3. When Peter was preaching at Pentecost,
   Walk in Jerusalem just like John,
   He was endowed with the Holy Ghost.
   Walk in Jerusalem just like John.

   [*to Refrain*]

I Want to Die Easy

Refrain:

I want to die easy when I die, when I die;
I want to die easy when I die, when I die;
I want to die easy when I die—
   Shout salvation as I fly;
I want to die easy when I die, when I die.

1. I want to see my mother when I die, when I die;
   I want to see my mother when I die, when I die;
   I want to see my mother when I die—
      Shout salvation as I fly;
   I want to see my mother when I die, when I die.

2. I want to see my Jesus when I die, when I die;
   I want to see my Jesus when I die, when I die;
   I want to see my Jesus when I die—
      Shout salvation as I fly;
   I want to see my Jesus when I die, when I die.

   [*to Refrain*]

Joshua Fought the Battle of Jericho

Refrain:

Joshua fought the Battle of Jericho,
Jericho, Jericho—
Joshua fought the Battle of Jericho,
And the walls came tumbling down.

You may talk about your king of Gideon,
You may talk about your man of Saul,
There's none like good old Joshua
At the Battle of Jericho.

    [*to Refrain*]

Up to the walls of Jericho
He marched with spear in hand;
"Go blow them ramhorns," Joshua cried,
"'Cause the battle is in my hands!"

    [*to Refrain*]

Then the lamb-ram-sheephorns began to blow,
Trumpets began to sound;
Joshua commanded the children to shout,
And the walls came tumbling down.
    That morning—

    [*to Refrain*]

Judgment Day Is Rolling 'Round

Refrain:

Judgment, Judgment,
Judgment Day is rolling 'round;
Judgment, Judgment,
O, how I long to go.

I've a good old mother in the heaven, my Lord,
    How I long to go there, too;
There's no back-sliding in the heaven, my Lord,
    How I long to go there, too.

King Jesus sitting in the heaven, my Lord,
    How I long to go there, too;
There's a big camp meeting in the heaven, my Lord,
    How I long to go there, too.

    [*to Refrain*]

Keep a-Inching Along

Keep a-inching along, keep a-inching along,
Master Jesus is coming by and by;
Keep a-inching along, keep a-inching along,
Master Jesus is coming by and by.

O, I died one time,
Going to die no more;
O, you in the Word,
And the Word in you;
How can I die when I'm in the Word?

Keep a-inching along, keep a-inching along,
Master Jesus is coming by and by;
Keep a-inching along, keep a-inching along,
Master Jesus is coming by and by.

Keep Me from Sinking Down

Refrain:

O Lord,
  O my Lord,
    O my good Lord,
Keep me from sinking down!

I tell you what I mean to do,
I mean to go to heaven, too;
I look up yonder, and what do I see?
I see the angels beckoning me.

  [*to Refrain*]

When I was a mourner just like you,
I mourned and mourned until I got through;
I bless the Lord, I'm going to die,
I'm going to Judgment by and by.

  [*to Refrain*]

Keep Your Lamps Trimmed and a-Burning

Keep your lamps trimmed and a-burning,
Keep your lamps trimmed and a-burning,
Keep your lamps trimmed and a-burning,
For this work's almost done.

Brothers, don't grow weary,
Brothers, don't grow weary,
Brothers, don't grow weary,
For this work's almost done.

'Tis religion makes us happy, *(etc.)*

We are climbing Jacob's ladder, *(etc.)*

Every round goes higher and higher, *(etc.)*

Keep your lamps trimmed and a-burning, *(etc.)*

Brothers, don't grow weary,
Brothers, don't grow weary,
Brothers, don't grow weary,
For this work's almost done.

Lay This Body Down

O, graveyard, O graveyard,
I'm walking through the graveyard;
　　Lay this body down.

I know moonlight, I know starlight,
I'm walking through the starlight;
　　Lay this body down.

I walk in the moonlight,
I walk in the starlight;
　　Lay this body down.

I know the graveyard,
I know the graveyard
　　When I lay this body down.

I lay in the graveyard
And stretch out my arms
　　When I lay this body down.

I go to the Judgment
In the evening of the Day,
　　When I lay this body down.

And my soul and your soul
Will meet in the Day
　　When I lay this body down.

Lead Me to the Rock

　　　O, lead me, lead me, my Lord,
　　　Lead me to the Rock that is higher than I;
　　　Lead me, lead me, my Lord,
　　　Lead me to the Rock that is higher than I.

1. The man who loves to serve the Lord
       Lead me to the Rock that is higher than I,
   Will surely get his just reward.
       Lead me to the Rock that is higher than I.

2. As I go down the stream of time,
       Lead me to the Rock that is higher than I,
   I leave this sinful world behind.
       Lead me to the Rock that is higher than I.

3. Old Satan's mad and I am glad,
       Lead me to the Rock that is higher than I,
   He missed the soul he thought he had.
       Lead me to the Rock that is higher than I.

       O, lead me, lead me, my Lord,
       Lead me to the Rock that is higher than I;
       Lead me, lead me, my Lord,
       Lead me to the Rock that is higher than I.

Let the Church Roll On

Let the church roll on,
    (Lord, Lord)
Let the church roll on,
    (Lord, Lord)
Let the church roll on,
    (Lord, Lord)
Let the church roll on.

Hypocrite in the church,
    (Lord, Lord)
Now that ain't right;
    (Lord, Lord)
Now what you gonna do?
    (Lord, Lord)
Let the church roll on.

    [responses continue as before]

If my brother has a fault,
    Let the church roll on.
If the liar has a fault,
    Bring him before the deacon.
If the deacon turns him out,
    Let the church roll on.
If that turn-back has a fault,
    Bring him before the elder.
If the elder turns him out,
    Let the church roll on.

Let the church roll on,
   (Lord, Lord)
Let the church roll on,
   (Lord, Lord)
Let the church roll on,
   (Lord, Lord)
Let the church roll on.

Let Us Break Bread Together

Let us break bread together on our knees;
Let us break bread together on our knees;
When I fall on my knees, with my face to the rising sun,
O Lord, have mercy on me.

Let us drink wine together on our knees;
Let us drink wine together on our knees;
When I fall on my knees, with my face to the rising sun,
O Lord, have mercy on me.

Let us praise God together on our knees;
Let us praise God together on our knees;
When I fall on my knees, with my face to the rising sun,
O Lord, have mercy on me.

Listen to the Lambs

   Listen to the lambs,
   Listen to the lambs,
   Listen to the lambs all a-crying,
   I want to go to heaven when I die.

1. Come on, sister, with your ups and downs,
       Want to go to to heaven when I die,
    Angels waiting for to give you a crown.
       Want to go to to heaven when I die.

2. Come on, sister, and don't be ashamed,
       Want to go to to heaven when I die,
    Angels waiting to write your name.
       Want to go to to heaven when I die.

3. Mind out, brother, how you walk the cross,
       Want to go to to heaven when I die,
    Foot might slip and your soul get lost.
       Want to go to to heaven when I die.

   Listen to the lambs,
   Listen to the lambs,
   Listen to the lambs all a-crying,
   I want to go to heaven when I die.

Lit'l Boy

"Lit'l Boy, how ole are you?
Lit'l Boy, how ole are you?
Lit'l Boy, how ole are you?"
"Sir, I'm only twelve years old."

This Lit'l Boy had them to remember
That He was born the twenty-fifth of December;
Lawyers and doctors were amazed,
And had to give the Lit'l Boy praise.

"Lit'l Boy, how ole are you?
Lit'l Boy, how ole are you?
Lit'l Boy, how ole are you?"
"Sir, I'm only twelve years old."

Lawyers and doctors stood and wondered,
As though they had been struck by thunder;
Then they decided while they wondered,
That all mankind must come under.

"Lit'l Boy, how ole are you?
Lit'l Boy, how ole are you?
Lit'l Boy, how ole are you?"
"Sir, I'm only twelve years old."

The last time the Lit'l Boy was seen,
He was standin' on Mount Olivet Green.
When He's dispersed of the crowd,
He entered up into a cloud.

"Lit'l Boy, how ole are you?
Lit'l Boy, how ole are you?
Lit'l Boy, how ole are you?"
"Sir, I'm only twelve years old."

Little David, Play on Your Harp
(1st version)

> *Refrain:*
>
> Little David, play on your harp,
>   Hallelu, hallelu!
> Little David, play on your harp,
>   Hallelu!

1. God told Moses,
    O Lord!
   "Go down in Egypt,
    O Lord!
   Tell old Pharaoh
    O Lord!
   Loose my people."
    O Lord!

   [*to Refrain*]

   [*responses and refrain continue as before*]

2. Down in the valley,
   Didn't go to stay;
   My soul got happy,
   I stayed all day.

3. Come down, angels,
   With ink and pen,
   And write salvation
   To dying men.

4. David had a harp,
   Had ten strings;
   Touch one string
   And the whole heaven ring.

5. I say to David,
   "Come play with me a piece."
   David said to me,
   "How can I play when I'm in a strange land?"

Little David, Play on Your Harp

(2nd version)

Little David, play on your harp, hallelujah!
Little David, play on your harp, hallelujah!
Little David, play on your harp, hallelu!

One day, one day I was walking along,
Yes, I heard a reason from on high,
Say, "Go in peace,
And sin no more;
Your sins are forgiven,
And your soul set free."

"I pluck your feet
Out of the miry clay
And set them on the rock of eternal age;
Where the wind may blow
And the storm may rise,
But the gates of hell
Shall never prevail."

Little David, play on your harp, hallelujah!
Little David, play on your harp, hallelujah!
Little David, play on your harp, hallelu!

Live Humble

Refrain:

Live humble, humble;
Humble yourselves, the bell's done rung;
Live humble, the bell's done rung.
    Glory and honor!
    Praise King Jesus!
    Glory and honor!
    Praise the Lord!

1. Watch that sun, how steady he runs,
   Don't let him catch you with your work undone.

   [*to Refrain*]

2. Ever see such a man as God?
   He gave up His Son for to come and die.

   [*to Refrain*]

3. Gave up His Son for to come and die,
   Just to save my soul from burning fire.

   [*to Refrain*]

4. See God 'n' you see God 'n' you see God in the morning,
   He'll come riding down the line of time.

   [*to Refrain*]

5. The fire'll be falling, He'll be calling,
   "Come to Judgment, come."

   [*to Refrain*]

Look How They Done My Lord

Look how they done my Lord,
Look how they done my Lord,
Look how they done my Lord,
O, look how they done my Lord,
    Done my Lord,
    Done my Lord,
    Done my Lord,
    Done my Lord.

[*the same repetitive patterns continue for each of the following lines*]

He never said a mumblin' word . . .
    They saw Him when He rise and fall . . .
        They carry Him to Calvary . . .
            He had to wear a thorny crown . . .
They carry Him to Pilate's hall . . .
    They licked Him with violence . . .
        Then they nailed Him to the tree . . .
The blood it come a-twinkling down . . .
    Thomas say, "I won't believe . . ."
        He said, "Thomas, see my hand . . ."
            He bowed His head and died.

Lord, How Come Me Here?

Lord, how come me here?
I wish I never was born.

There ain't no freedom here, Lord.
I wish I never was born.

They treat me so mean here, Lord.
I wish I never was born.

They sold my children away, Lord.
I wish I never was born.

Lord, how come me here?
I wish I never was born.

Lord, I Want to Be a Christian

Refrain:

Lord, I want to be a Christian
In my heart, in my heart;
Lord, I want to be a Christian
In my heart, in my heart.

1. Lord, I want to be more loving
   In my heart, in my heart, *(etc.)*

2. Lord, I want to be more holy
   In my heart, in my heart, *(etc.)*

3. Lord, I don't want to be like Judas
   In my heart, in my heart, *(etc.)*

4. Lord, I want to be like Jesus
   In my heart, in my heart, *(etc.)*

   [*to Refrain*]

Many Thousand Gone

No more auction block for me,
No more, no more;
No more auction block for me,
Many thousand gone.

No more peck of corn for me . . . *(etc.)*
   No more driver's lash for me . . .
      No more pint of salt for me . . .
         No more hundred lash for me . . .
            No more mistress' call for me . . .

Mary and Martha

Mary and Martha just gone 'long,
Mary and Martha just gone 'long,
Mary and Martha just gone 'long
To ring them charming* bells.

Crying free grace and dying love,
Free grace and dying love,
Free grace and dying love,
To ring them charming bells.

O! 'Way over Jordan, Lord,
'Way over Jordan, Lord,
'Way over Jordan, Lord,
To ring them charming bells.

The preacher and the elder's just gone 'long, *(etc.)*

My father and my mother's just gone 'long, *(etc.)*

The Methodist and the Baptist's just gone 'long, *(etc.)*

*dialect for "chiming"

Mary and Martha just gone 'long,
Mary and Martha just gone 'long,
Mary and Martha just gone 'long
To ring them charming bells.

Mary Had a Baby

Mary had a baby,
 Yes, Lord!
Mary had a baby,
 Yes, Lord!
Mary had a baby,
 Yes, Lord!
The people keep a-comin'
And the train done gone.

What did she name Him?
 Yes, Lord!
What did she name Him?
 Yes, Lord!
What did she name Him?
 Yes, Lord!
The people keep a-comin'
And the train done gone.

She name Him King Jesus, *(etc.)*

She name Him Mighty Counselor, *(etc.)*

Where was He born?, *(etc.)*

He was born in a manger, *(etc.)*

My God Is So High

 My God is so high, you can't get over Him;
 He's so low, you can't get under Him;
 He's so wide, you can't get around Him—
 You must come in, by, and through the Lamb.

One day as I was walking along the heavenly road,
My Saviour spoke unto me, and He filled my heart with love.

 O, He's so high, you can't get over Him;
 He's so low, you can't get under Him;
 He's so wide, you can't get around Him—
 You must come in, by, and through the Lamb.

I tell you, fellow members, things happen mighty strange;
The Lord was good to Israel, and His way don't ever change.

O, He's so high, you can't get over Him;
He's so low, you can't get under Him;
He's so wide, you can't get around Him—
You must come in, by, and through the Lamb.

My Good Lord's Been Here

[The similarly titled "The Lord's Been Here," p. 82, carries a different structure, text and music.]

Refrain:

My good Lord's been here,
Been here, been here;
My good Lord's been here,
And He's blessed my soul and gone.

1. O brothers, where were you?
   Brothers, where were you?
   Brothers, where were you
   When my good Lord was here?

   [*to Refrain*]

2. O sisters, where were you? *(etc.)*

3. O Christians, where were you? *(etc.)*

4. O mourners, where were you? *(etc.)*

My Lord Says He's Going to Rain Down Fire

Refrain:

My Lord, my Lord,
My Lord says He's going to rain down fire;
My Lord, my Lord,
My Lord says He's going to rain down fire.

1. Pharaoh, Pharaoh,
   Pharaoh and his host got drowned.
      My Lord, my Lord,
      My Lord says He's going to rain down fire.

2. Gabriel, Gabriel,
   Gabriel, blow your silver trumpet.
      My Lord, my Lord,
      My Lord says He's going to rain down fire.

3. Peter, Peter, Peter on the Sea of Galilee,
   Take your net and follow me.
         (etc.)

4. Moses, Moses, Moses smote the Red Sea over;
Moses, Moses, Moses smote the Red Sea over.
  (etc.)

[*to Refrain*]

My Lord's Writing All the Time

Come down, come down, my Lord, come down,
And take me up to wear the crown!

King Jesus rides in the middle of the air,
He's calling sinners from everywhere!

My Lord's writing all the time,
My Lord's writing all the time;
O, He sees all you do, hears all you say,
My Lord's writing all the time.

When I was down in Egypt's land,
I heard some talk of the Promised Land;
Christians, you had better pray,
For Satan's 'round you every day.

My Lord's writing all the time,
My Lord's writing all the time;
O, He sees all you do, hears all you say,
My Lord's writing all the time.

My Lord! What a Mourning

Refrain:

My Lord! what a mourning,
My Lord! what a mourning,
My Lord! what a mourning
When the stars begin to fall.

1. You'll hear the trumpets sound to wake
The nations underground,
Looking to my God's right hand
When the stars begin to fall.

[*to Refrain*]

2. You'll hear the sinner cry to wake
The nations underground,
Looking to my God's right hand
When the stars begin to fall.

[*to Refrain*]

3. You'll hear the Christian shout to wake
   The nations underground,
   Looking to my God's right hand
   When the stars begin to fall.

   [*to Refrain*]

My Soul's Been Anchored in the Lord

Refrain & Response:

O, my soul's been anchored in the Lord,
   Ain't you glad!
My soul's been anchored in the Lord,
   Can't you sing it!
My soul's been anchored in the Lord,
   Tell it, children!
My soul's been anchored in the Lord.

Verse & Response:

1. Where've you been, poor sinner?
      O, I'm happy!
   Where've you been so long?
      Found my Jesus!
   Been working out of the sight of man,
      On my knees!

   [*to Refrain*]

2. You may talk about me just as much as you please,
      You can't hurt me!
   You may spread my name abroad,
      For I'm sheltered!
   I'll pray for you when I get on my knees,
      In my Jesus!

   [*to Refrain*]

3. See my father in the gospel
      Left my burden
   Come wagging up the hill so slow,
      At the river,
   He's crying now as he cried before.
      In the valley!

   [*to Refrain*]

My Way Is Cloudy

Refrain:

Oh, brethren, my way,
    My way's cloudy, my way;
        Go send them angels down.
Oh, brethren, my way,
    My way's cloudy, my way;
        Go send them angels down.

There's fire in the East and fire in the West,
And fire among the Methodists;
Old Satan's mad and I am glad,
He missed the soul he thought he had.

    [*to Refrain*]

I'll tell you now as I told you before,
To the Promised Land I'm bound to go;
This is the year of Jubilee,
The Lord has come to set us free.

    [*to Refrain*]

Nobody Knows the Trouble I See
(1st version)

Refrain:

Nobody knows the trouble I see, Lord,
Nobody knows but Jesus;
Nobody knows the trouble I see,
Glory, hallelujah!

1. Sometimes I'm up, sometimes I'm down;
    O yes, Lord!
Sometimes I'm almost on the ground.
    O yes, Lord!

    [*to Refrain*]

2. Although you see me going 'long so,
    O yes, Lord!
I have my troubles here below.
    O yes, Lord!

    [*to Refrain*]

3. One day I was walking along,
    O yes, Lord!
The element opened and the love came down.
    O yes, Lord!

    [*to Refrain*]

4. I shall never forget that day,
    O yes, Lord!
When Jesus washed my sins away.
    O yes, Lord!

    [*to Refrain*]

Nobody Knows the Trouble I See
(2nd version)

Refrain:

Nobody knows the trouble I see, Lord,
Nobody knows the trouble I see, Lord,
Nobody knows the trouble I see, Lord,
Nobody knows like Jesus.

1. Brothers, will you pray for me?
Brothers, will you pray for me?
Brothers, will you pray for me,
And help me to drive old Satan away?

    [*to Refrain*]

2. Sisters, will you pray for me? *(etc.)*

3. Mothers, will you pray for me? *(etc.)*

4. Preachers, will you pray for me? *(etc.)*

O, Brothers, Don't Get Weary

O, brothers, don't get weary,
O, brothers, don't get weary,
O, brothers, don't get weary,
We're waiting for the Lord.

We'll land on Canaan's shore,
We'll land on Canaan's shore,
When we land on Canaan's shore
We'll meet forevermore.

O, Freedom

O, freedom,
    O, freedom,
        O, freedom over me!
And before I'd be a slave,
    I'll be buried in my grave,
        And go home to my Lord and be free.

No more moaning,
　　No more moaning,
　　　　No more moaning over me!
No more weeping,
　　No more weeping,
　　　　No more weeping over me!

　　(There'll be singing over me!)

There'll be shouting,
　　There'll be shouting,
　　　　There'll be shouting over me!
There'll be praying,
　　There'll be praying,
　　　　There'll be praying over me.

O, freedom,
　　O, freedom,
　　　　O, freedom over me!
And before I'd be a slave,
　　I'll be buried in my grave,
　　　　And go home to my Lord and be free.

O, Gambler, Get Up Off Your Knees!

O, gambler, get up off your knees,
O, gambler, get up off your knees,
O, gambler, get up off your knees!
　　End of that morning, good Lord,
　　End of that morning, good Lord,
　　End of that morning when the Lord said to hurry.

O, gambler, you can't ride on this train,
O, gambler, you can't ride on this train,
O, gambler, you can't ride on this train!
　　End of that morning, good Lord,
　　End of that morning, good Lord,
　　End of that morning when the Lord said to hurry.

O, Glory!

Refrain:

O, Glory!
There's room enough in Paradise
　　To have a home in Glory!

There's room enough in Paradise
To have a home in Glory!
Jesus, my all, to heaven is gone
To have a home in Glory!
He whom I fix my hopes upon
To have a home in Glory!

[*to Refrain*]

His track I see and I'll pursue
To have a home in Glory!
The narrow way 'til Him I view
To have a home in Glory!

[*to Refrain*]

Old Ship of Zion

1. What ship is that a-sailing, Hallelujah,
   What ship is that a-sailing, Hallelu!
   'Tis the old ship of Zion, Hallelujah,
   'Tis the old ship of Zion, Hallelu!

   Do you think that she is able, Hallelujah,
   Do you think that she is able, Hallelu!
   Do you think that she is able
   For to carry us all home?
       O, glory, Hallelu!

2. She has landed many a thousand, Hallelujah,
   She has landed many a thousand, Hallelu!
   She has landed many a thousand,
   And will land as many more.
       O, glory, Hallelu!

3. She is loaded down with angels, Hallelujah,
   She is loaded down with angels, Hallelu!
   And King Jesus is the Captain,
   And He'll carry us all home.
       O, glory, Hallelu!

O, Lord, Have Mercy on Me

Yes, we'll all fall on our knees
And face the rising sun;
Yes, we'll all fall on our knees
And face the rising sun.
    O, Lord, have mercy on me.

If we never pray together anymore,
If we never pray together anymore,
Yes, we'll all fall on our knees
And face the rising sun.
O, Lord, have mercy on me.

If we never meet together anymore,
If we never groan together anymore,
If we never preach together anymore,
Yes, we'll all fall on our knees
And face the rising sun.
O, Lord, have mercy on me.

O, Lord, Hear Me Praying

Lord, O hear me praying, Lord,
O, hear me praying, Lord,
O, hear me praying;
    I want to be more holy every day,
    O, I want to be more holy every day.

Like Peter, when you said to him,
"Feed my sheep, feed my lambs."
    Lord, O hear me praying, Lord,
    (etc.)

Like Peter, when you said to him,
"I build my church upon this rock,
O, the gates of hell will never shock."
    Lord, O hear me praying, Lord,
    (etc.)

Like Jesus when he said to me,
"I am the voice;
Everyday come out the wilderness
To prepare the way."
    Lord, O hear me praying, Lord,
    (etc.)

O, Mary, Don't You Weep

O, Mary, don't you weep, don't you moan,
O, Mary, don't you weep, don't you moan;
Pharaoh's army already got drowned,
O, Mary, don't you weep.

One of these mornings bright and fair,
Gonna take my wings and cleave the air;
Pharaoh's army already got drowned,
O, Mary, don't you weep.

O, Po' Little Jesus

Refrain:

O, po' little Jesus, O, po' little Jesus,
O, po' little Jesus, this world gonna break Your heart;
There'll be no place to lay Your head, my Lord.

O, Mary she bow down and cry,
O, Mary she bow down and cry,
For there's no place to lay His head.

O, po' little Jesus, O, po' little Jesus, *(etc.)*

Come down, all you holy angels,
Sing 'round Him with your golden harps,
For some day He will die to save this world.

O, po' little Jesus, O, po' little Jesus, *(etc.)*

O, Rocks, Don't Fall on Me!

Refrain:

O, rocks, don't fall on me,
O, rocks, don't fall on me,
O, rocks, don't fall on me,
Rocks and mountains, don't fall on me!

Look over yonder on Jericho's wall,
   Rocks and mountains, don't fall on me!
And see those sinners tremble and fall.
   Rocks and mountains, don't fall on me!

[*to Refrain*]

In-a that great, great Judgment Day
   Rocks and mountains, don't fall on me!
The sinners will run to the rocks and say:
   Rocks and mountains, don't fall on me!

[*to Refrain*]

When every star refuses to shine,
   Rocks and mountains, don't fall on me!
I know that King Jesus will be mine.
   Rocks and mountains, don't fall on me!

[*to Refrain*]

The trump shall sound, and the dead shall rise,
   Rocks and mountains, don't fall on me!
And go to the mansions in-a the skies.
   Rocks and mountains, don't fall on me!

[*to Refrain*]

Over the Crossing

Bending knees a-aching, body racked with pain,
I wish I was a child of God,
    I'd get home by and by.
Keep praying, I do believe
We've a long time wagging over the crossing;
Keep praying, I do believe
    We'll get home to heaven by and by.

O, yonder's my old mother,
Been a-wagging at the hill so long,
It's about time she crossed over,
    Get home by and by.

O, hear that lumbering thunder
A-roll from door to door,
A-calling the people home to God;
    They'll come home by and by.

O, see that forked lightning
A-jump from cloud to cloud,
A-picking up God's children;
    They'll get home by and by.

Pray, mourner, I do believe,
Little children, I do believe
    We'll get home to heaven by and by.

O, What a Beautiful City

O, what a beautiful city,
Twelve gates a-to the city,
Hallelu.

Three gates in-a the East,
Three gates in-a the West,
Three gates in-a the North,
Three gates in-a the South,
That makes twelve gates a-to the city,
Hallelu.

O, what a beautiful city *(etc.)*

My Lord built that city,
Said it was just a-four square;
Said he wanted you sinners
To meet him in-a the air
'Cause there's twelve gates a-to the city,
Hallelu.

O, what a beautiful city *(etc.)*

Three gates, three gates,
Then three gates plus three more gates
Makes twelve gates a-to the city,
Hallelu.

Peter, Go Ring Them Bells

O, Peter, go ring them bells,
O, Peter, go ring them bells,
Peter, go ring them bells,
I heard from heaven today.

I wonder where my mother's gone,
I wonder where sister Mary's gone,
I wonder where sister Martha's gone,
I wonder where brother Moses' gone,
I wonder where brother Daniel's gone,
He's gone where Elijah has gone.

It's good news, and I thank God,
I heard from heaven today.
O, Peter, go ring them bells,
I heard from heaven today.

Plenty Good Room
(1st version)

Refrain:

There's plenty good room,
There's plenty good room,
'Way in the kingdom;
There's plenty good room,
There's plenty good room,
'Way in the kingdom.

1. My Lord's done just what He said,
   'Way in the kingdom,
   Healed the sick and raised the dead,
   'Way in the kingdom.

2. One of these mornings bright and fair,
   'Way in the kingdom,
   Going to hitch on my wings and cleave the air,
   'Way in the kingdom.

3. When I was a mourner just like you,
   'Way in the kingdom,
   I prayed and prayed 'til I came through,
   'Way in the kingdom.

4. Come on, mourner, make a bound,
    'Way in the kingdom,
The Lord will meet you on halfway ground,
    'Way in the kingdom.

    Refrain:

    There's plenty good room,
        There's plenty good room,
            'Way in the kingdom;
    There's plenty good room,
        There's plenty good room,
            'Way in the kingdom.

Plenty Good Room
(2nd version)

    Refrain:

    Plenty good room, plenty good room,
    Good room in my Father's kingdom;
    Plenty good room, plenty good room,
    Just choose your seat and sit down.

1. I would not be a sinner,
    I tell you the reason why:
    'Cause if my Lord should call on me,
    I wouldn't be ready to die.

    [to Refrain]

2. I would not be a back-slider,
    I tell you the reason why:
    'Cause if my Lord should call on me,
    I wouldn't be ready to die.

    [to Refrain]

Poor Me

1. I'm sometimes up, I'm sometimes down,
    Trouble will bury me down,
    But still my soul feels heavenly bound,
    Trouble will bury me down.
        O, brethren!—

    Refrain:

    Poor me, poor me,
    Trouble will bury me down;
    Poor me, poor me,
    Trouble will bury me down.

2. Hallelujah to the Lamb,
    Trouble will bury me down,
   The Lord is on the giving hand,
    Trouble will bury me down.
        O, brethren!—

    [*to Refrain*]

3. Sometimes I think I'm ready to drop,
    Trouble will bury me down,
   But, thank my Lord, I do not stop,
    Trouble will bury me down.
        O, brethren!—

    [*to Refrain*]

Poor Mourner's Got a Home at Last

My Lord! My Lord!
Poor mourner's got a home at last!

1. O, mourner, mourner, ain't you tired a-mourning?
   Bow down on your knees and join the band with the angels.
        No harm, no harm,
        Go tell brother Elijah;
            No harm, no harm,
            Poor mourner's got a home at last.

2. O, sinner, sinner, ain't you tired a-sinning?
   Bow down on your knees and join the band with the angels.
        No harm, no harm,
        Go tell brother Elijah;
            No harm, no harm,
            Poor mourner's got a home at last.

3. O, gambler, gambler, ain't you tired a-gambling?
   Bow down on your knees and join the band with the angels.
        No harm, no harm, *(etc.)*

4. O, seeker, seeker, ain't you tired a-seeking?
   Bow down on your knees and join the band with the angels.
        No harm, no harm, *(etc.)*

5. O, preacher, preacher, ain't you tired a-preaching?
   Bow down on your knees and join the band with the angels.
        No harm, no harm, *(etc.)*

Ride On, King Jesus!

(1st version)

[This popular spiritual exists in three versions known to the editors. The single—and singular—difference between versions 1 and 2 centers on the odd shift from "Him" to "me" in the line "No man can hinder (Him/me)." The 2nd version, following this one, is written out in its entirety. The concluding 3rd version has a significantly different text.]

Refrain:

Ride on, King Jesus!
No man can hinder Him;
Ride on, King Jesus!
No man can hinder Him.

1. King Jesus rides on a milk-white horse,
   No man can hinder Him,
   The river of Jordan He did cross.
   No man can hinder Him.

   [*to Refrain*]

2. If you want to find your way to God,
   No man can hinder Him,
   The gospel highway must be trod.
   No man can hinder Him.

   [*to Refrain*]

3. I was young when I begun,
   No man can hinder Him,
   But now my race is almost run.
   No man can hinder Him.

   [*to Refrain*]

Ride On, King Jesus!

(2nd version)

Refrain:

Ride on, King Jesus!
No man can a-hinder me;
Ride on, King Jesus!
No man can a-hinder me.

1. I was but young when I begun,
   No man can a-hinder me,
   But now my race is almost done.
   No man can a-hinder me.

   [*to Refrain*]

2. King Jesus rides on a milk-white horse,
   No man can a-hinder me,
The river of Jordan He did cross.
   No man can a-hinder me.

   [*to Refrain*]

3. If you want to find your way to God,
   No man can a-hinder me,
The gospel highway must be trod.
   No man can a-hinder me.

   [*to Refrain*]

Ride On, King Jesus!
(3rd version)

Ride on, King Jesus, ride on—
   No man can ever work like Him.
Ride on, King Jesus, ride on!

Why, He's the King of Kings and Lord of Lords,
Jesus Christ, the first and last—
   No man can ever work like Him.

I will not let You go, my Lord,
Until You come and bless my soul—
   No man can ever work like Him.

King Jesus rides on a milk-white horse—
   No man can ever work like Him.
For Paul and Silas bound in jail—
   No man can ever work like Him.
The Christians prayed both day and night—
   No man can ever work like Him.

Ride on, King Jesus, ride on—
He's the King of Kings and Lord of Lords!
Ride on, King Jesus, ride on—
   No man can ever work like Him.

Ride the Chariot

   Refrain:

   Ride the chariot in the morning,
   Lord, ride the chariot in the morning,
   Lord, ride the chariot in the morning,
   Lord, I'm gonna ride the chariot in the morning.

Lord, I'm getting ready for the Judgment Day,
    My Lord, my Lord,
I'm getting ready for the Judgment Day,
    My Lord, my Lord.

    [*to Refrain*]

Are you ready, my brother,
    Are you ready for the journey?
Are you ready, my sister,
    Are you ready for the journey?

    [*to Refrain*]

Do you want to see your Jesus?
    Do you want to see your Jesus?
O, yes, I'm waiting for the chariot
    'Cause I'm ready to go.

    [*to Refrain*]

I never can forget that day
    When all my sins were taken away;
I'll serve my Lord 'til Judgment Day;
    Ride the chariot to see my Lord,
    Ride the chariot in the morning, Lord.

    [*to Refrain*]

Rise and Shine

O, brethren, rise and shine,
And give God the glory, glory;
    Rise and shine,
    And give God the glory, glory;
        Rise and shine,
        And give God the glory for the years of Jubilee.

Don't you want to be a soldier, soldier, soldier?
Don't you want to be a soldier, soldier, soldier?
Do you think I will make a soldier?
Yes, I think you will make a soldier for the year of Jubilee!

O, brethren, rise and shine,
And give God the glory, glory;
    Rise and shine,
    And give God the glory, glory;
        Rise and shine,
        And give God the glory for the years of Jubilee.

'Rise! Shine! for Thy Light Is Coming!

Refrain:

O, 'rise! shine! for thy light is coming!
'Rise! shine! for thy light is coming!
O 'rise! shine! for thy light is coming,
My Lord says He's coming by and by!

This is the year of Jubilee,
My Lord has set his people free;
I intend to shout and never stop
Until I reach the mountaintop!

[*to Refrain*]

Wet or dry, I intent to try
To serve the Lord until I die.

[*to Refrain*]

Rise Up, Shepherd, and Follow!

There's a star in the East on Christmas morn,
Rise up, shepherd, and follow!
It'll lead to the place where the Saviour's born.
Rise up, shepherd, and follow!

Take good heed to the Angel's word,
Rise up, shepherd, and follow!
You'll forget your flock, you'll forget your herd.
Rise up, shepherd, and follow!

Leave your flocks and leave your lambs,
Rise up, shepherd, and follow!
Leave your sheep and leave your rams.
Rise up, shepherd, and follow!

Follow . . . Follow . . .
Rise up, shepherd, and follow!
Follow the Star of Bethlehem.
Rise up, shepherd, and follow!

Rock-a My Soul

(1st version)

Refrain:

Rock-a my soul in the bosom of Abraham,
Rock-a my soul in the bosom of Abraham,
Rock-a my soul in the bosom of Abraham,
O, rock-a my soul!

71

1. I never shall forget the day
   When Jesus washed my sins away!
   [*to Refrain*]

2. I know my God is a man of war;
   He fought my battle at hell's dark door!
   [*to Refrain*]

   [*verse-refrain pattern continues as before*]

3. If you don't believe I'm a child of God,
   Follow me where the road is hard!

4. One day, one day I was walking nigh—
   Yes, I heard a reason from on high!

5. I remember the day, I remember it well—
   My sins were forgiven and my soul saved from hell!

6. I went down to the valley, and didn't go to stay;
   My soul got happy and I stayed all day!

7. Just look up yonder at what I see—
   A band of angels coming after me!

8. If you get there before I do,
   Tell my Lord I'm coming, too!

9. When I get to heaven and sit right down,
   I'll ask my Lord for my starry crown!

Rock-a My Soul

(2nd version)

[According to one source, the two *stanzas* of this version are almost identical to the *refrain* of the spiritual "My God Is So High" (p. 54).]

Refrain:

Rock-a my soul in the bosom of Abraham,
Rock-a my soul in the bosom of Abraham,
Rock-a my soul in the bosom of Abraham,
O, rock-a my soul!

1. My Lord is so high, you can't get over Him;
   So low, you can't get under Him;
   So wide, you can't get around Him—
   You must go in at the door!

   [*to Refrain*]

2. His love is so high, you can't get over it;
   So low, you can't get under it;
   So wide, you can't get around it—
   You must go in at the door!

   [*to Refrain*]

72

Roll, Jordan, Roll

Refrain:

Roll, Jordan, roll;
Roll, Jordan, roll;
I want to go to heaven when I die
To hear old Jordan roll.

1. O, brothers, you ought to have been there,
   Yes, My Lord!
   A-sitting in the kingdom, to hear Jordan roll.

   [*to Refrain*]

2. O, preachers, you ought to have been there,
   Yes, My Lord!
   A-sitting in the kingdom, to hear Jordan roll.

   [*to Refrain*]

3. O, sinners, you ought to have been there, *(etc.)*

4. O, mourners, you ought to have been there, *(etc.)*

5. O, seekers, you ought to have been there, *(etc.)*

6. O, mothers, you ought to have been there, *(etc.)*

7. O, sisters, you ought to have been there, *(etc.)*

Run, Mourner, Run!

1. There's singing here,
   There's singing there;
   I believe down in my soul
   There's singing everywhere.

   Refrain:

   Run, mourner, run!
   Lo! says the Bible.
   Run, mourner, run!
   Lo! is the way.

2. There's preaching here,
   There's preaching there;
   I believe down in my soul
   There's preaching everywhere.

   [*to Refrain*]

3. There's praying here,
   There's praying there;
   I believe down in my soul
   There's praying everywhere.

   [*to Refrain*]

Singing with a Sword in My Hand

Prettiest singing ever I heard,
'Way over on the hill—
The angels sing, and I sing, too.

    Singing with a sword in my hand, Lord,
    Singing with a sword in my hand;
    Singing with a sword in my hand, Lord,
    Singing with a sword in my hand.

Prettiest shouting ever I heard,
'Way over on the hill—
The angels shout, and I shout, too.

    Shouting with a sword in my hand, Lord,
    Shouting with a sword in my hand;
    Shouting with a sword in my hand, Lord,
    Shouting with a sword in my hand.

Prettiest preaching ever I heard,
'Way over on the hill—
The angels preached, and I preached, too.

    Preaching with a sword in my hand, Lord,
    Preaching with a sword in my hand;
    Preaching with a sword in my hand, Lord,
    Preaching with a sword in my hand.

Prettiest mourning ever I heard,
'Way over on the hill—
The angels mourned, and I mourned, too.

    Mourning with a sword in my hand, Lord,
    Mourning with a sword in my hand;
    Mourning with a sword in my hand, Lord,
    Mourning with a sword in my hand.

Sinner, Please Don't Let This Harvest Pass

Refrain:

Sinner, please don't let this harvest pass,
Sinner, please don't let this harvest pass,
Sinner, please don't let this harvest pass,
    And die and lose your soul at last.

1. I know that my Redeemer lives,
   I know that my Redeemer lives,
   I know that my Redeemer lives;
       Sinner, please don't let this harvest pass.

   [*to Refrain*]

2. Sinner, O see the cruel tree,
   Sinner, O see the cruel tree,
   Sinner, O see the cruel tree
       Where Christ died for you and me.

   [*to Refrain*]

3. My God is a mighty man of war,
   My God is a mighty man of war,
   My God is a mighty man of war;
       Sinner, please don't let this harvest pass.

   [*to Refrain*]

Sister Mary Had But One Child

Refrain:

Sister Mary had but one Child,
Born in Bethlehem;
And every time the Baby cried
She rocked Him in the weary land.

1. Three wise men to Jerusalem came,
   They'd travelled very far;
   They said, "Where is He born, King of the Jews?
   For we have seen His star."

   King Herod's heart was troubled,
   He marvelled but his face was grim;
   He said, "Tell me where the Child may be found,
   I'll go and worship Him."

   [*to Refrain*]

2. An angel appeared to Joseph
   And gave him this command:
   "Arise ye, take your wife and child,
   Go flee into Egypt land.

   "For yonder comes old Herod,
   A wicked man and bold;
   He's slaying all the children
   From six to eight days old,
   From six to eight days old."

   [*to Refrain*]

Sit Down, Servant, Sit Down!

Refrain:

Sit down, servant, sit down!
Sit down, servant, sit down!
Sit down, servant, sit down!
Sit down and rest a little while.

1. I know you mighty tired,
       So sit down;
   Know you mighty tired,
       So sit down.

   [*to Refrain*]

2. I know you shoutin' happy,
       So sit down;
   Know you shoutin' happy,
       So sit down.

   [*to Refrain*]

3. You come over mountain, *(etc.)*

4. I know you had trouble, *(etc.)*

5. I know you been crying, *(etc.)*

6. I know you been praying, *(etc.)*

7. I know you been afflicted, *(etc.)*

8. It's a tiresome journey, *(etc.)*

9. It's a long journey, *(etc.)*

Sometimes I Feel Like a Motherless Child

[The refrain is omitted in some variants of this spiritual.]

Sometimes I feel like a motherless child,
Sometimes I feel like a motherless child,
Sometimes I feel like a motherless child,
    Far, far away from home,
    A long, long ways from home;
    True believer—a long ways from home.

    Refrain:

    Then I get down on my knees and pray,
    Get down on my knees and pray.

Sometimes I feel like I'm almost gone,
Sometimes I feel like I'm almost gone,
Sometimes I feel like I'm almost gone,
    'Way up in the heavenly land,
    'Way up in the heavenly land,
    True believer—'way up in the heavenly land,

    [*to Refrain*]

If this was Judgment Day,
If this was Judgment Day,
If this was Judgment Day,
    Every little soul would pray,
    Every little soul would pray,
    True believer—every little soul would pray.

    [*to Refrain*]

Soon I'll Be Done

(1st version)

Soon I'll be done with the troubles of this world,
Soon I'll be done with the troubles of this world,
Soon I'll be done with the troubles of this world,
    Going to live with God.

Come, my brother, go with me,
Come, my brother, go with me,
Come, my brother, go with me,
    Let King Jesus make you free.

When I get to heaven, I will sing and tell,
When I get to heaven, I will sing and tell,
When I get to heaven, I will sing and tell
    How I did shun both death and hell.

Soon-a Will Be Done-a

(2nd version)

> *Refrain:*
>
> Soon-a will be done-a with the troubles of the world,
> Troubles of the world, the troubles of the world;
> Soon-a will be done-a with the troubles of the world,
> Goin' home to live with God.

1. No more weeping and a-wailing,
    No more weeping and a-wailing,
    No more weeping and a-wailing,
    I'm goin' to live with God.

    [to Refrain]

2. I want to meet my mother,
    I want to meet my mother,
    I want to meet my mother,
    I'm goin' to live with God.

    [to Refrain]

3. I want to meet my Jesus,
    I want to meet my Jesus,
    I want to meet my Jesus,
    I'm goin' to live with God.

    [to Refrain]

Stand Still, Jordan

Stand still, Jordan,
Stand still, Jordan,
Stand still, Jordan,
Lord, I can't stand still.

I got a mother in heaven,
I got a mother in heaven,
I got a mother in heaven,
Lord, I can't stand still.

When I get up in glory,
When I get up in glory,
When I get up in glory,
Lord, I can't stand still.

Jordan river, Jordan river,
Jordan river is chilly and cold.
It will chill my body,
It will chill my body,
It will chill my body,
But not my soul.

Steal Away to Jesus

Steal away, steal away,
Steal away to Jesus!
Steal away, steal away home,
I ain't got long to stay here.

My Lord calls me:
He calls me by the thunder;
The trumpet sounds within my soul;
I ain't got long to stay here.

My Lord calls me:
He calls me by the lightning;
The trumpet sounds within my soul;
I ain't got long to stay here.

Green trees are a-bending:
Poor sinners stand a-trembling;
The trumpet sounds within my soul;
I ain't got long to stay here.

Tombstones are a-bursting:
Poor sinners are a-trembling;
The trumpet sounds within my soul;
I ain't got long to stay here.

Steal away, steal away,
Steal away to Jesus!
Steal away, steal away home,
I ain't got long to stay here.

Sweet Heaven

Heaven, sweet heaven,
O, Lord, I want to go to heaven!
Heaven, sweet heaven,
O, Lord, I want to go to heaven!

You lie on me, they lie on you,
Lie on everybody;
The last lie you told on me,
It's gonna raise me higher in heaven.

Heaven, sweet heaven,
O, Lord, I want to go to heaven!
Heaven, sweet heaven,
O, Lord, I want to go to heaven!

Ezekiel saw the mighty big wheel:
In the big wheel there was a little wheel;
The big wheel stands for God Himself,
And the little wheel stands for Jesus Christ.

Heaven, sweet heaven,
O, Lord, I want to go to heaven!
Heaven, sweet heaven,
O, Lord, I want to go to heaven!

Sweet Home

Refrain:

Sweet home, sweet home,
Sweet home, sweet home,
Lord, I wonder if I'll ever get home.

I heard the voice of Jesus say,
"Come unto me and rest;
Lay down, thy weary one,
Lay down down thy head upon my breast."

[*to Refrain*]

I came to Jesus as I was—
Weary, worn and sad,
And I found in Him a resting place,
And He has made me glad.

[*to Refrain*]

Swing Low, Sweet Chariot

(popular version)

Refrain:

Swing low, sweet chariot,
Coming for to carry me home;
Swing low, sweet chariot,
Coming for to carry me home.

1. I looked over Jordan, and what did I see,
       Coming for to carry me home?
    A band of angels coming after me,
       Coming for to carry me home.

    [*to Refrain*]

2. If you get there before I do,
       Coming for to carry me home,
    Tell all my friends I'm coming, too,
       Coming for to carry me home.

    [*to Refrain*]

80

3. The brightest day that ever I saw,
    Coming for to carry me home,
When Jesus washed my sins away,
    Coming for to carry me home.

    [*to Refrain*]

4. I'm sometimes up, and sometimes down,
    Coming for to carry me home,
But still my soul feels heavenly bound,
    Coming for to carry me home.

    [*to Refrain*]

Swing Low, Sweet Chariot
[Good Old Chariot]
(alternate version)

Swing low, sweet chariot,
Swing low, sweet chariot,
Swing low, sweet chariot—
    Don't you leave me behind,
    O, don't you leave me behind.

Good old chariot, swing low,
Good old chariot, swing low,
Good old chariot, swing low—
    Don't you leave me behind,
    O, don't you leave me behind.

Good old chariot, take us all home,
Good old chariot, take us all home,
Good old chariot, take us all home—
    Don't you leave me behind,
    O, don't you leave me behind.

The Angels Done Bowed Down

    Refrain:

O, the angels done bowed down,
O, the angels done bowed down,
O, the angels done bowed down,
O, yes, my Lord!

While Jesus was hanging upon the cross,
The angels kept quiet till God went off;
And the angels hung their harps on the willow trees
To give satisfaction till God was pleased.

    [*to Refrain*]

His soul went up on the pillar of cloud,
O, God he moved and the angels did bow;
Jehovah's sword was at His side,
On the empty air He began to ride.

[*to Refrain*]

"Go down, angels, to the flood,
Blow out the sun, turn the moon into blood!
Come back, angels, bolt the door,
The time that's been will be no more!"

[*to Refrain*]

The Angels Rolled the Stone Away

Refrain:

The angels rolled the stone away,
The angels rolled the stone away;
'Twas a bright and shiny morn
When the trumpet began to sound;
The angels rolled the stone away,
The angels rolled the stone away.

1. Sister Mary came running at the break of day,
   Brought the news from heaven:
   "I'm looking for my Saviour,
   Tell me where He lay—
   High up on the mountain
   The stone done rolled away."

   [*to Refrain*]

2. The soldiers were a-plenty,
   Standing by the door;
   But they could not hinder
   The stone done rolled away.

   [*to Refrain*]

3. Old Pilate and his wise men
   Didn't know what to say—
   The miracle was on them,
   The stone done rolled away.

The Lord's Been Here
[The similarly titled "My Good Lord's Been Here," p. 55, carries a different structure, text and music.]

The Lord's been here and blessed my soul,
The Lord's been here and blessed my soul,
   O glory!
The Lord's been here and blessed my soul,
The Lord's been here and blessed my soul.

I ain't gonna lay my religion down,
I ain't gonna lay my religion down,
O glory!
I ain't gonna lay my religion down,
I ain't gonna lay my religion down.

Gonna shoulder up my cross,
Gonna shoulder up my cross,
O glory!
Gonna shoulder up my cross,
Gonna shoulder up my cross.

There's a Meeting Here Tonight

Refrain:

Get you ready—
There's a meeting here tonight;
Come along—
There's a meeting here tonight;
I know you by your daily walk—
There's a meeting here tonight.

1. Camp-meeting down in the wilderness,
   There's a meeting here tonight
   I know it's among the Methodists,
   There's a meeting here tonight.

   [*to Refrain*]

2. Those angel wings are tipped with gold,
   There's a meeting here tonight
   That brought glad tidings to my soul,
   There's a meeting here tonight.

   [*to Refrain*]

3. My father says it is the best
   There's a meeting here tonight
   To live and die a Methodist,
   There's a meeting here tonight.

   [*to Refrain*]

4. I'm a Methodist bred, and a Methodist born,
   There's a meeting here tonight
   And when I'm dead, there's a Methodist gone,
   There's a meeting here tonight.

   [*to Refrain*]

There's No Hiding Place Down There

There's no hiding place down there,
There's no hiding place down there,
    O, I went to the rock to hide my face,
    But the rock cried out, "No hiding place!"—
There's no hiding place down there.

O, the rock cried, "I'm burning, too,"
O, the rock cried, "I'm burning, too,"
    O, the rock cried, "I'm burning, too,
    I want to go to heaven as well as you!"—
There's no hiding place down there.

O, the sinner man, he gambled and fell,
O, the sinner man, he gambled and fell,
    O, the sinner man, he gambled and fell,
    He wanted to go to heaven but he had to go to hell—
There's no hiding place down there.

They Led My Lord Away

Refrain:

They led my Lord away, away, away,
They led my Lord away—
O, tell me where to find Him.

1. The Jews and Romans in one band,
    Tell me where to find Him,
  They crucified the Son of Man,
    Tell me where to find Him.

    [to Refrain]

2. They led Him up to Pilate's bar,
    Tell me where to find Him,
  But they could not condemn Him there,
    Tell me where to find Him.

    [to Refrain]

3. Old Pilate said, "I wash my hands,"
    Tell me where to find Him,
  "I find no fault in this just man."
    Tell me where to find Him.

    [to Refrain]

This Train

This train is bound for glory, this train!
This train is bound for glory, this train!
    This train is bound for glory,
    This train is bound for glory,
This train is bound for glory, this train!

This train don't haul no gamblers, this train! *(etc.)*

This train don't haul no extras, this train! *(etc.)*

This train don't haul no sinners, this train! *(etc.)*

Tone the Bell

    Tone the bell—
        Done got over,
    Tone the bell—
        Done got over,
    Tone the bell—
        Done got over,
        Done got over at last.

Old Satan's like a snake in the grass,
    Tone the bell—
        Done got over,
Always in a Christian's path!
    Tone the bell—
        Done got over,
        Done got over at last.

Old Satan shot his ball at me,
    Tone the bell—
        Done got over,
He missed my soul and caught my sins!
    Tone the bell—
        Done got over,
        Done got over at last.

[*the next verses follow the same pattern*]

Old Satan's mad, and I am glad . . .
I trust the Lord I'm gonna keep him mad!

Old Satan thought he had me fast . . .
But I broke his chain and got free at last!

Sister, you better mind how you walk on the cross . . .
Your foot might slip and your soul get lost.

What makes me praise my Lord so bold . . .
He washed my sins as white as snow.

To See God's Bleedin' Lamb

Want to go to heaven when I die,
When I die, when I die;
Want to go to heaven when I die
To see God's bleedin' Lamb.

Jacob's ladder deep and long,
Deep and long, deep and long;
Jacob's ladder deep and long
To see God's bleedin' Lamb.

See God's angels comin' down
To see God's bleedin' Lamb;
Comin' down in a sheet of blood
To see God's bleedin' Lamb.

Sheet of blood all mingle' with fire
To see God's bleedin' Lamb;
Then you raise your voice up higher
To see God's bleedin' Lamb;
An' you join the heavenly Choir
To see God's bleedin' Lamb.

Trying to Get Home

Lord, I'm bearing heavy burdens
    Trying to get home;
Lord, I'm bearing heavy burdens
    Trying to get home;
Lord, I'm bearing heavy burdens
    Trying to get home.

Lord, I'm climbing high mountains
    Trying to get home;
Lord, I'm climbing high mountains
    Trying to get home;
Lord, I'm climbing high mountains
    Trying to get home.

Lord, I'm standing hard trials
    Trying to get home;
Lord, I'm standing hard trials
    Trying to get home;
Lord, I'm standing hard trials
    Trying to get home.

Two Wings

Lord, I want two wings to veil my face,
I want two wings for to fly away;
Lord, I want two wings to veil my face,
I want two wings for to fly away.

O, meet me, Jesus, meet me—
Meet me in the air;
And if these two wings fail me,
Just give me another pair.

Lord, I want two wings to veil my face,
I want two wings for to fly away;
Lord, I want two wings to veil my face,
I want two wings for to fly away.

Until I Reach My Home

Until I reach my home,
Until I reach my home,
I never intend to give the journey over
Until I reach my home.

O, some say, "Give me silver!"
And some say, "Give me gold!"
But I say, "Give me Jesus,
Most precious to my soul."

Until I reach my home,
Until I reach my home,
I never intend to give the journey over
Until I reach my home.

They say that John the Baptist
Was nothing but a Jew;
But the Holy Bible tells us
That he was a preacher, too.

Until I reach my home,
Until I reach my home,
I never intend to give the journey over
Until I reach my home.

Up on the Mountain

'Way up on the mountain,
    Lord!
I heard God talking.
    Lord!
Children—the chariot stopped.
    Lord!
One day,
    Lord!
One day,
    Lord!
Walking 'long,
    Lord!
With hung-down head,
    Lord!
Children—an aching heart.
    Lord!

Walk in Jerusalem, Just Like John

Last Sunday morning! Last Sunday morning!
    Walk in Jerusalem, just like John;
    Walk in Jerusalem, all God's people;
    Walk in Jerusalem, tell the angels;
    Walk in Jerusalem, just like John.

Train is a-coming! train is a-coming!
    Walk in Jerusalem, just like John;
    Walk in Jerusalem, all my brethren;
    Walk in Jerusalem, all my sisters;
    Walk in Jerusalem, just like John.

She is loaded down with angels! Loaded down with angels!
    Walk in Jerusalem, just like John;
    Walk in Jerusalem, see my father;
    Walk in Jerusalem, see my mother;
    Walk in Jerusalem, just like John.

Walk, Mary, Down the Lane

Three long nights and three long days,
    Jesus walking down the lane;
        Three long nights and three long days,
        Jesus walking down the lane.

In the morning, down the lane;
    In the morning, down the lane;
        In the morning, down the lane;
        In the morning, down the lane.

Walk, Mary, down the lane;
   Walk, Mary, down the lane;
      Walk, Mary, down the lane;
         Walk, Mary, down the lane.

Jesus calls you down the lane, *(etc.)*

In the heaven, down the lane, *(etc.)*

'Fraid nobody, down the lane, *(etc.)*

Walk, Mary, down the lane, *(etc.)*

Walk Together, Children

Walk together, children,
   Don't you get weary;
Walk together, children,
   Don't you get weary;
O, talk together, children,
   Don't you get weary—
There's a great camp-meeting in the Promised Land.

Sing together, children,
   Don't you get weary;
Sing together, children,
   Don't you get weary;
O, shout together, children,
   Don't you get weary—
There's a great camp-meeting in the Promised Land.

   Gone to mourn and never tire,
   Mourn and never tire,
   Mourn and never tire,
   There's a great camp-meeting in the Promised Land.

O, get you ready, children,
   Don't you get weary;
Get you ready, children,
   Don't you get weary;
We'll enter there, O children,
   Don't you get weary—
There's a great camp-meeting in the Promised Land.

Wasn't That a Wide River

Refrain:

   O, wasn't that a wide river,
   River of Jordan, Lord! Wide river!
   There's one more river to cross,
   One more river to cross.

O, the river of Jordan is so wide,
I don't know how to get on the other side;
I have some friends before me gone,
By the grace of God, I'll follow on.

[*to Refrain*]

Shout! Shout! Satan's about!
Shut your door and keep him out!
Old Satan is a snake in the grass,
If you don't mind, he'll get you at last!

[*to Refrain*]

We Are Climbing Jacob's Ladder

1. We are climbing Jacob's ladder,
   We are climbing Jacob's ladder,
   We are climbing Jacob's ladder,
   Soldiers of the cross.

2. Ev'ry round goes higher, higher,
   Ev'ry round goes higher, higher,
   Ev'ry round goes higher, higher,
   Soldiers of the cross.

3. Brother, do you love my Jesus?
   (*etc.*)

4. If you love Him, you must serve Him,
   (*etc.*)

5. We are climbing higher, higher,
   (*etc.*)

Were You There When They Crucified My Lord?

1. Were you there when they crucified my Lord?
   (Were you there?)
   Were you there when they crucified my Lord?
   Oh!—
   Sometimes it causes me to tremble, tremble, tremble—
   Were you there when they crucified my Lord?

2. Were you there when they nailed Him to the tree?
   (Were you there?)
   Were you there when they nailed Him to the tree?
   Oh!—
   Sometimes it causes me to tremble, tremble, tremble—
   Were you there when they nailed Him to the tree?

3. Were you there when they pierced Him in the side? (*etc.*)

4. Were you there when the sun refused to shine? *(etc.)*

5. Were you there when they laid Him in the tomb? *(etc.)*

What You Gonna Do When the Lamp Burns Down?

O, poor sinner, now is your time,
O, poor sinner, now is your time.
What you gonna do when the lamp burns down?

O, the lamp burned down and you can't see,
O, the lamp burned down and you can't see.
What you gonna do when the lamp burns down?

Ezekiel saw that wheel of time,
And every spoke was of humankind.
What you gonna do when the lamp burns down?

God made man and made him out of clay,
And put him on the earth, but not to stay.
What you gonna do when the lamp burns down?

They cast old Daniel in the lion's den,
And Jesus locked the lion's jaw.
What you gonna do when the lamp burns down?

Old Satan's mad and I am glad;
He missed one soul he thought he had.
What you gonna do when the lamp burns down?

Old Satan's a liar and a conjurer, too;
If you don't mind, he'll slip it on you!
What you gonna do when the lamp burns down?

O, poor sinner, now is your time,
O, poor sinner, now is your time.
What you gonna do when the lamp burns down?

When I Fall on My Knees

Let us break bread together
　　On our knees,
　　Yes, on our knees;
Let us break bread together
　　On our knees,
　　Yes, on our knees;
When I fall on my knees
With my face to the rising sun,
O, Lord, have mercy on me.

Let us drink wine together
    On our knees,
      Yes, on our knees;
Let us drink wine together
    On our knees,
      Yes, on our knees;
When I fall on my knees
With my face to the rising sun,
O, Lord, have mercy on me.

Let us praise God together
    On our knees,
      Yes, on our knees;
Let us praise God together
    On our knees,
      Yes, on our knees;
When I fall on my knees
With my face to the rising sun,
O, Lord, have mercy on me.

When the Saints Go Marching In

(1st version)

1. O, when the saints go marching in,
   O, when the saints go marching in,
   Lord, I want to be in that number
   When the saints go marchin' in.

2. O, when they come on Judgment Day,
   O, when they come on Judgment Day,
   Lord, I want to be in that number
   When they come on Judgment Day.

3. When Gabriel blows that golden horn,
   When Gabriel blows that golden horn,
   Lord, I want to be in that number
   When he blows that golden horn.

4. When they go through them Pearly Gates,
   When they go through them Pearly Gates,
   Lord, I want to be in that number
   When they go through Pearly Gates.

5. O, when they ring them silver bells,
   O, when they ring them silver bells,
   Lord, I want to be in that number
   When they ring them silver bells.

6. And when the angels gather 'round,
   And when the angels gather 'round,
   Lord, I want to be in that number
   When the angels gather 'round.

7. O, into Heaven when they go,
O, into Heaven when they go,
How I want to be in that number
Into Heaven when they go.

8. And when they're singing "Hallelu,"
And when they're singing "Hallelu,"
How I want to be in that number
When they're singing "Hallelu."

9. And when the Lord is shakin' hands,
And when the Lord is shakin' hands,
How I want to be in that number
When the Lord is shakin' hands.

When the Saints Go Marching In
(2nd version)

When the saints go marching in,
When the saints go marching in,
Lord, I want to be in that number
When the saints go marching in!

1. I have a loving brother,
He is gone on before—
And I promised I would meet him
When they crown Him Lord of all.

When they crown Him Lord of all,
When they crown Him Lord of all,
When they crown Him Lord of all,
Lord, I want to be in that number
When they crown Him Lord of all!

2. I have a loving sister,
She is gone on before—
And I promised I would meet her
When they gather 'round the throne.

When they gather 'round the throne,
When they gather 'round the throne,
Lord, I want to be in that number
When they gather 'round the throne.

Witness

(1st version)

Leader & Chorus:

My soul is a witness
    For my Lord,
My soul is a witness
    For my Lord,
My soul is a witness
    For my Lord,
My soul is a witness
    For my Lord.

1. You read in the Bible and you understand,
Methuselah was the oldest man;
He lived nine hundred and ninety-nine,
He died and went to heaven, Lord, in a-due time.

   Now Methuselah was a witness for my Lord,
   Methuselah was a witness for my Lord,
   Methuselah was a witness for my Lord,
   Methuselah was a witness for my Lord.

2. You read in the Bible and you understand,
You read in the Bible and you understand,
Samson went out at a-one time,
And he killed about a thousand of the Philistines.

   Delilah fooled Samson, this we know,
   For the Holy Bible tells us so;
   She shaved off his head just as clean as your hand,
   And his strength became as any other man's.

   Now Samson was a witness for my Lord,
   Samson was a witness for my Lord,
   Samson was a witness for my Lord,
   Samson was a witness for my Lord.

3. Now Daniel was a Hebrew child,
He went to pray to his Lord awhile;
The King at once for Daniel did send,
And he put him right down in the lion's den.
God sent his angels the lions for to keep,
And Daniel lay down and went to sleep.

   Now Daniel was a witness for my Lord,
   Daniel was a witness for my Lord,
   Daniel was a witness for my Lord,
   Daniel was a witness for my Lord.

Who will be a witness for my Lord?
Who will be a witness for my Lord?
Who will be a witness for my Lord?
Who will be a witness for my Lord?

Witness

(2nd version)

Oh, Lord, what manner of man is this?
All nations in Him are blessed;
All things are done by His will;
He spoke to the sea and the sea stood still.

    Now, ain't that a witness for my Lord?
    Ain't that a witness for my Lord?
    Ain't that a witness for my Lord?
    My soul is a witness for my Lord.

Now, there was a man of the Pharisees,
His name was Nicodemus and he didn't believe.
The same came to Christ by night,
Wanted to be taught out of human sight.

Nicodemus was a man desired to know
How a man can be born when he is old.
Christ told Nicodemus, as a friend,
"Man, you must be born again."

Said, "Marvel not, man, if you wanna be wise,
Repent, believe, and be baptized."
Then you'll be a witness for my Lord;
My soul is a witness for my Lord.

Now, you read about Samson, from his birth
Strongest man that ever lived on earth;
'Way back yonder in ancient times
He killed ten thousand of the Philistines.

Then old Samson went wanderin' about;
Samson's strength was never found out
'Til his wife sat upon his knee.
She said, "Tell me where your strength lies, if you please."

Now, Samson's wife, she talk so fair,
Samson said, "Cut off-a my hair.
Shave my head as clean as your hand
And my strength will become like a natural man."

    Old Samson was a witness for my Lord.
    My soul is a witness for my Lord.
    There's another witness,
    My soul is a witness for my Lord!

You Can Tell the World

Refrain:

You can tell the world about this,
You can tell the nation about that—
Tell 'em what Jesus has done!
Tell 'em that the Comforter has come!
And He brought joy, great joy to my soul.

Well, He took my feet on the miry clay,
Yes, He did!
And He place them on the rock to stay.
Yes, He did!

[*to Refrain*]

Well, you know, my Lord done just what He said—
Yes, He did!
He healed the sick and He raised the dead.
Yes, He did!

[*to Refrain*]

You'd Better Run

You'd better run, run, run-a-run,
You'd better run, run, run-a-run;
You'd better run to the city of refuge,
You'd better run, run, run.

God sent old Jonah to the Ninevah land,
He didn't obey my God's command;
The wind blew the ship from shore to shore,
A whale swallowed Jonah and he wasn't no more.

He had to run, run, run-a-run,
He'd better run, run, run-a-run;
He'd better run to the city of refuge,
He'd better run, run, run.

Read about Samson from his birth
He was the strongest man on earth;
He lived 'way back in ancient times,
He killed about a thousand Philistines.

He had to run, run, run-a-run,
He'd better run, run, run-a-run;
He'd better run to the city of refuge,
He'd better run, run, run.

You Go, I'll Go With You

You go, I'll go with you,
Open your mouth, I'll speak for you;
Lord, if I go, tell me what to say,
They won't believe in me.

Lord, I give myself away,
'Til all that I can do;
If Thou withdraw Thyself from me,
Oh, whither shall I go?

The archangels don' droop their wings,
Went on Zion hill to sing;
Now, you go, I'll go with you,
Open your mouth, I'll speak for you;
Lord, if I go, tell me what to say,
They won't believe in me.

You Got a Right

You got a right, I got a right,
We all got a right to the tree of life—
Yes, tree of life.

The very time I thought I was lost,
The dungeon shook and the chain fell off.
You may hinder me here,
But you can't hinder me there
'Cause God in the heaven's
Going to answer prayer.

O, brother, O, sister,
You got a right, I got a right,
We all got a right to the tree of life—
Yes, tree of life.

You Hear the Lambs a-Cryin'

Refrain:

You hear the lambs a-cryin',
Hear the lambs a-cryin',
Hear the lambs a-cryin',
O, Shepherd, feed my sheep.

1. My Saviour spoke these words so sweet,
   O, Shepherd, feed my sheep,
   Saying, "Peter, if you love me, feed my sheep."
   O, Shepherd, feed my sheep.

   [*to Refrain*]

2. Lord, I love Thee, Thou dost know,
   O, Shepherd, feed my sheep,
   O, give me grace to love Thee more.
   O, Shepherd, feed my sheep.

   [*to Refrain*]

[*the remaining verses continue the same pattern
of statement-response-refrain*]

3. I don't know what you want to stay here for,
   For this vain world's no friend to grace.

4. If I only had wings like Noah's dove,
   I'd fly away to the heavens above.

5. When I am in an agony,
   When you see me, pity me.

6. For I am a pilgrim travelling on
   The lonesome road where Jesus gone.

7. O, see my Jesus hanging high,
   He looked so pale, and bled so free.

8. O, wasn't that an awful shame?
   He hung three hours in mortal pain.

Your Low-Down Ways

Your low-down ways, your low-down ways,
God's going to get you about your low-down ways,
God's going to get you about your low-down ways.

You talk about your elder when he's tryin' to preach the word;
You talk about your neighbor when he's trying to praise the Lord;
You talk about your sister when she's on her knees praying.

Your low-down ways, your low-down ways,
God's going to get you about your low-down ways,
God's going to get you about your low-down ways.

You Shall Reap Just What You Sow

You shall reap just what you sow,
You shall reap just what you sow;
On the mountain, in the valley,
You shall reap just what you sow.

Brother, sister, sinner,
You shall reap just what you sow;
On the mountain, in the valley,
You shall reap just what you sow.